Consider the Damn Lily

Essays About Life with
God, Humanity, and the F Word

SUSAN DUTY

For Lorene, Mary, and Ava

DAMMIT, EILEEN! WHERE'D YOU PUT THAT ESSAY?

II. HOLD FAST TO DREAMS

IV. CLEOPATRA

V. HOLD EVEN FASTER TO DREAMS BECAUSE WE'RE GOING BROKE

VI. WELL, SINCE WE'RE AMONG THE LIVING

VII. POEMS THAT I DON'T CALL POEMS

VIII. GOD IS NOT A SENATOR

ACKNOWLEDGMENTS

The most profound thanks is extended to Mr. Jim McKeown, high-ranking member of the Grammar Police, a fraternal order established on the moss-covered stone floor of a castle now often visited by hipsters and D&D enthusiasts in Edinburgh, Scotland.

I'd also be remiss if I didn't thank the Lady of St. Louis/San Antonio/probably a million other places, Lisa McCollough, for her unfailing support – moral, professional, and otherwise.

Another warm expression of gratitude is owed to the following people for their input, advice, shoulders to cry on, encouragement, metaphorical slaps to the face, and hope-filled high-fives:

Roland Duty – a king in his own right, Leanna Moss, Louie Daisy Love, Brookey Brooke and the Funky Bunch, Summer Shine, Ashley V., Auntie Jen, Linda (last name unknown), Chris, Suanne G., Jan C., Stephanie Campbell, Wino Chuck, Big James, and thousands of other wonderful human beings.

1. A VERY GOOD PLACE TO START

Fuck.

Let's get it out of the way. There'll be a lot more of it in the following pages. I do love and believe in a God, but for whatever reason, I still say that word a lot. I suppose it's because the gutter is a second home to me, and of course everybody in the gutter cusses. Maybe the world is one big gutter. Even the suburbs. Even the ones in a fancy town like Houston.

I have an emotional gutter and a spiritual gutter. It's slimy and gross and full of wiggly, crawly things like anger and pride and selfishness. I hang with people who acknowledge their own dark, hidden inner sewer, too. We talk about how it looks and ways to stop piling trash in one corner and just let God have His way with our messes.

I'm not one to touch slime anyway.

Spirituality is one big, funky trip. Some people think they know something about it, and others admit they know nothing. Some think it's all a made-up lie by powerful men who want to drive Cadillacs they can write off on their taxes.

Some are mad at a God they say they don't believe in. Some are blissfully confused and content in that confusion because it gives them a righteous rock from which they point and stare at all the other sinful people, especially ones who say fuck a lot.

I'm of the school who believes I don't know much. The second I think I know something or finally get it, a new revelation throws my other epiphanies off the table and I'm left standing with my mouth agape.

Damn it. Again?

Yes, again. Each time.

My latest thought is that I can't know anything about spirituality really. Spirituality is an experience. It's all experience. The stars in the cosmos don't contemplate their deeper meaning. They just burn and explode with a precision quickness and illuminate a blackness that calls me to wonder. They simply "are." A star does what a star does best, and I am made of stars. I am the cosmos. I am everything.

That's all we have, too. All we have in this game is experience. It is our invaluable currency with each other. That's why I think it's important that you share it as often as possible however you can. If you write music, sing about your experience. If you're a writer, write about it. If you're an accountant, stop for five seconds and see how you can share what you've been through with someone who is in the thick of it.

It will help you tremendously. More than that, it will help all of us, too.

I was raised in a nice, big church that had a drummer and an organist. Worship was a real show and I remember liking it. The sermon part was a different situation. I remember almost immediately thinking God was very unhappy with me. He knew I had a gutter and He sure didn't approve of all the trash piling up in my little 10-year-old spirit.

I thought those people who looked so nice didn't have what I had. They didn't have trash. They had nice SUVs and white dresses. They had headbands with flowers on them and Lacoste shirts. They were wholesome and perfect. They fit in to the Church, and I knew I didn't. I just didn't want to be found out because I'd miss all the singing.

It didn't help that I started doing illicit drugs in large quantities and drinking to blackout. Point is, I have a pleasant mix of gutter and glory. And you know what? So does everyone else.

It's important for you to know a few things from Jump Street, because the stories that follow don't run on a timeline. Ready? Here we go.

I had a gnarly run with drugs and alcohol that landed me in jail and the nuthouse a few times. After a few brushes with death, I got sober on March 7, 2008. I was twenty-two years old. It is still a significant date to me and I celebrate every year in my own way.

I was married and divorced twice before turning 32. The first was to a nice guy in the military when I was 19. The second was to a rather unkind man at 29. In between those two marriages, I got pregnant, almost a year to the day that I got sober. I was never, as so many people assume, married to my daughter's father. I was with him just about long enough to make a baby.

The second marriage was abusive, mostly mental and emotional. It's significant enough for me to mention it because it took up a substantial portion of my sober life and had a profound effect on me when it finally ended.

5

I was able to buy a house during that marriage, which I chalked up as a victory because my former house was so small and sort of run down. I had finally constructed a dreamy life for myself, or at least it looked that way on the outside. Yikes. It was a nightmare really. But isn't that the way it always goes? That guy put me in therapy and a boxing class – but not in the same year.

This narrative, if I may be so bold, is published here in the hopes it will reach the minds of other humans struggling and trudging in their attempt to navigate this sometimes crappy, lonely, dark, dismal, depressing sphere of rock and water.

Some of these essays recount specific experiences of mine. Others describe feelings and thoughts I have on various topics. I hope you find them enjoyable. I hope you find them helpful.

If you are easily offended, this may be the time you silently curse yourself for wasting the purchase price of this book. If you are at the jumping off place, this may be your gate. And lucky you, there's no security checkpoint and I don't want to do a body scan on you. Come as you are. Let's party.

At the end, I encourage you to pass this book along to another person you think might benefit from it. I hope when the wheels touch down on your encounter with these pages, you realize we're all on the same plane going to the same destination. It'll make this dump a lot less lonely.

Cross-check and all-call, prepare for departure. Please stay seated until the captain has turned off the seatbelt sign. And remember, there is no smoking in the lavatories.

I.

THIS NEXT PART IS A LITTLE FUZZY

2. THIRTY-FIVE FEET

A Long Island Ice Tea and electricity is a horrible combination.

Taser guns emit 50,000 volts of electricity and can be fired at a distance of 35 feet. I'd consumed enough liquor that particular night to limit my remembrance of how far away from the officer I was, but I do know that I was in that 35-foot range when two metal prongs snaked themselves into the skin of my elbow on the side of I-35.

The morning of October 11, 2006 was normal. The word is used real loosely here. I'd decided to go down to Austin to look at sound equipment because in my alcohol-soaked mind I thought it was really time to get that independent film production company up and running. I didn't want to go alone obviously, so I invited my sister to tag along.

Somehow, we never made it to any kind of sound equipment store, but did happen to find a hipster taco place where they served daquiris at noon to dreamers like me. I had plenty of money at this point in my life. I was finally 21 and I could drink legally in public places. It just made sense. The afternoon daquiri birthed the idea of going to 6th Street, Austin's premier drunk tank.

A pub on the corner proved the perfect place to post up in my black, polka dot swing dress and peep-toe heels. I would fit in here. I would be welcomed like a Spartan returning from war. I chatted with the bartender about Johnny Cash as I sipped my beer, my underage sister sitting nearby. Shots became a good idea, and I felt the ego-driven diva well up inside me, declaring my ability to hang with the guys while still acting like a lady. Nope. I turned into an inebriated version of Andy Dick with a lot more creepiness, if you can believe that.

The very last drink I remember ordering was a Long Island Ice Tea. Anyone who considers themselves an alcoholic can't resist one. It doesn't need a selling point other than: It has basically every kind of alcohol on earth in it. Boom. Sign me up! Let's go to the moon! I remember walking around the bar, holding my drink like I built the place with my bare hands. I talked to a few tables I think... or maybe I just walked up to them and openly drooled because I was no longer the master of my bodily functions.

There was a homeless man I remember talking to outside. I sobbed over his story and vowed to help him somehow. By this point, my sister had run to get the car and was dragging me out of the place where everyone surely loved me. The next flash of remembered thought was of me coming to in the car and throwing up all over the place. Maybe I made a wrong choice? We may never know.

I don't remember this part, but what I was told later was that I began swinging violently in the car. My sister, fearing for both our lives as she drove, pulled over on the side of the interstate to see if she could talk some sense into me. Nope. I got out and began running around the highway. I punched her, and she returned the favor. This was evidenced by the swollen lip I have in my mugshot. I had grown 100% uncontainable, and because she thought she was going to watch her sister go head to head with an 18-wheeler and lose in the middle of the busy road, she made the decision to call for help.

Good Lord and they showed up.

I used to watch a lot of the show, *Cops*. I still love it, but I don't have cable so I don't see much of any TV. I'm pretty sure the fluid surrounding the tender tissue of my brain was just pure rum at this point, and so when I saw the Williamson Country Sheriff's Department show up, logic mixed with TV and I took off running the opposite direction. I fell in a ditch because like a jackass I didn't think to take off my fucking high heels while I attempted to evade arrest.

They were quicker than me and nabbed me just in time. I was handcuffed and thrown into the back of my first squad car. The seats were so hard. Hey guys, let's go for padded seats in the next bond election.

They discussed something outside, probably with my sister who was trying to explain the situation to them. I didn't much care for being handcuffed when all I really wanted to do was smoke the joint hidden in my pack of cigarettes. I began kicking the window as hard as I could as I laid in the plastic seats with my hands behind my back.

Then, I became a fucking genius again.

I remember seeing videos about how to break a window should your car ever take a tumble into a lake and you need to make an escape. *If I hit the window in the center with my heel, it should shatter.* But first I'd need to get these cuffs off me.

When you're drunk, your body can do all kinds of things it normally can't. Apparently when I'm drunk, my wrists become bird legs because I slid those damn things right off and took to kicking the window again, now empowered by my master plan to blow this joint. I kicked and **CRASH**. The window broke. I reached my hand through the shattered glass, opened the door, and let myself the hell on out.

I ran again and fell *of course* because I still hadn't taken my shoes off. Also, I was a wee bit trashed. Putting together the night is hard when you blackout because it's like a shitty patchwork quilt that doesn't make sense. You have to construct a timeline for yourself and there are these huge blocks of time where apparently your body was working, but your brain was like, "nah." So, the next little patch of fabric in the shitty quilt my night was becoming was just me hearing the arresting officer yell: "Stand back! I'm going to deploy the taser!"

This phrase alone is enough to bring you right out of unconsciousness. I remember feeling like I was ready to give up, but that guy had apparently been chasing me for the better part of twenty minutes and he was kind of tired of it. And when you get tasered, your body immediately quits working. I went from a dead sprint to a face plant in the grass along I-35 in Georgetown, Texas. Oh, the humanity.

The next several moments I remember very clearly because they're burned into my frontal lobe like a sick etch-a-sketch that no one ever shakes. To put it in a word: *Fuuuuuuuuuuuuuuck!!!* To put it in two nicer ones: *Please stop!!* Eventually, the sheriff let his finger off the trigger. An EMT removed the prongs from my elbow and I was unceremoniously thrown into the back of another squad car with two intact windows. Off to the jail we went. I was brought in, fingerprinted, and then put in a padded dress in a cell by myself. Booking number 246955. I wasn't foaming at the mouth or anything, but they, too, knew my brain was swimming in rum. Couldn't take any chances.

That was another one of the nights I almost died when I was a chemical-drenched psychopath. And to think, later I became a public school teacher. That was always an inside joke between God and me because up until this moment, I had never told anyone about that story. Well, I told a few people who are like me in a lot of ways because I knew they wouldn't judge me for it. Hell, they'd done it, too, once or twice.

I feel like everyone should have that experience at least once. Everyone should drink way too much liquor and make really bad choices and ride an electric wave controlled by an authority figure much more powerful than you. If you can't arrange that or that idea doesn't sound appealing, go drink three-quarters of a handle of vodka and get on a rollercoaster. The effect will be about the same, just maybe less shattered glass and misdemeanors involved.

3. MERRY CHRISTMAS! THIS IS A LOCKDOWN WARD.

A drunken stunt gone horribly wrong was the threshold of what would prove to be the end.

Christmas is the most magical time of the year. Everyone is happy and everything smells like pine. People don't count calories and no one judges you for eating a whole pie. And then there are the entire days spent inside drinking beer and Robitussin so you can avoid smoking weed and blowing probation. Hey man, they can't drug test you for dextromethorphan.

Ah, shit. Yes they can!

I didn't know it, but the crazy train I had been riding since the summer before my freshman year of high school was coming to an end. I was about to come face to face with what a lot of people like to call a "bottom." It was Christmas Eve, so I was more concerned about drinking beer to celebrate Jesus than maybe eating a little food that day. Food wasn't always a big priority at that point in life, but to celebrate the birth of the Savior, one must consume a bit of turkey with the ones they love.

Every day in the last year of my drinking was spent relatively the same. I woke up. I drank. I picked up my husband from work and was yelled at for driving drunk. We went home. We fought. I passed out. Every day. I did try to not drink sometimes towards the end. Maybe I'd wake up and say, "Not today, Susan." And then I'd sit on the couch and rock back and forth, flipping through channels on the TV trying to distract myself long enough until the overwhelming feeling of wanting to drink left. But that Beast was so powerful that I'd only last an hour or two before I threw in the towel on trying to make a better life for myself. It had kicked my ass and demanded payment. I'd grab my wallet and my keys and head to the liquor store that was within walking distance of my house.

I don't think I had attempted sobriety this day. It was the Holidays! So anyway, there I am, all lit up and my husband and I are fighting. I thought, *I'm going to run around the block because you make me so angry*! We were fighting about how much I drank and how I was a nightmare to be around. Gah, like I killed the mayor or something. In typical downer-fueled, drama queen fashion, I sprinted out the front door and down the dark street at full blast crazy. I got maybe a half a mile down the road before I realized this wasn't going to get my point across. Don't know what my point was, but I knew it was important and people needed to listen to it and understand me.

Bam! Back in the door I flew. This time, though, I knew what I was going to do. *I'm going to take a knife and I'm going to cut on myself just a little bit, just enough to draw some blood, and everyone is going to just shut the hell up about all this drinking business.* I went to the kitchen and ripped open the utensil drawer. I grabbed this little knife – well, what I thought was little. I set it to my wrist, pressed down probably a little too hard, and then raked its blade across my skin. I went "across the river" and not down, which should have been evidence enough that it wasn't a sincere suicide attempt. But physiology didn't care.

Blood immediately sprayed onto the floor. The blade completed its swift trip across my forearm, and I

15

knew I had done something terrible and irreversible. My husband came in to see what I had done. I went from rage to weak in a matter of seconds. I had trouble standing and blood continued to flow from my very open wound. He got on the phone and called 911, telling them I had slit my wrist trying to kill myself. *I'll sort out the details later*, I thought. That wasn't my intention.

I had been a cutter for a long time actually. I don't remember the first time I did it. I don't remember where I learned about it. But at some point in my adolescence, I initiated myself into a club of people who probably know pain more intimately than others. I cut for two reasons: 1) to punish myself for a crime I had been convicted of by the prosecutor who lives in my head, and 2) to stop the hurricane of emotion that would form in my chest during times of great struggle. Anything sharp would do usually. Maybe it was a pair of scissors or maybe a knife. I remember shattering a picture one time and saving some of the glass because it had worked so efficiently when I used it to rid myself of the remorse I felt after breaking something so dear.

People who don't cut or engage in self-harm don't get it. And hey, I don't blame you. That shit ain't right! But to people who know, it makes sense. I never liked doing it. I never looked forward to it. It was always just a means to an end for me. I guess some people pray when they get into a jam and others go to the gym. For me, when things got bad, I liked to take sharp objects and slide them across my skin just hard enough to let my blood flood to the top in the hopes my brain would release enough endorphins to bring me back down to reality. Yes, it's sick. I don't need you to tell me that.

It was this understanding that led me to do what I did. If I could get enough blood to come out, he'd realize my drinking wasn't a useful topic of discussion, and I'd be left to do what I wanted. That's some selfish bullshit, isn't it? I know.

He took a shirt of his that I had ripped in a physical altercation earlier off the floor where it was still lying and made a makeshift tourniquet to stop the bleeding. He'd completed two tours in Iraq and this was part of his training. Then he walked me very slowly to the living room so we could wait for the ambulance. My feet were lifted and placed on a box in front of a wall by the door. I laid there, quiet, still, and scared for a while. I stared at the wall in front of me.

Suddenly, there was what appeared to be a surgeon's lamp above my head. Maybe it was more like those lights they have at the dentist's office – you know, the ones they shove in your face so they can clean your teeth. It was bright but didn't quite take up my whole field of vision. A blanket of peace covered me all over and I felt whole and blissfully content. That sounds pretty nuts considering the circumstances.

I kept gazing at the light, completely mesmerized, and slowly it began to expand. It started to push out all the black that was surrounding it. I guess people would say I was in a sort of trance. And it wasn't just the light I was looking at. There was the peace. If I could figure out a way to get that back I would. It was probably the calmest I have ever been in my entire life – including the time in my sobriety. Now I know it's not scary when you die.

My husband told me later that at about that time he started slapping my face, telling me to not go to sleep. I wasn't going to sleep! I was chilling on the floor looking at this beautiful glow and feeling as mellow as a human can feel! There was then a knock at the door and all the feelings and the light evaporated. There was just the wall again. Bummer.

The EMT leaned down and looked at my arm. He complimented my husband on his tourniquet. Then he asked me, "Ma'am, have you been drinking?"

What an idiot. First of all, bro, who does this sober? Ok, plenty of people. Well second of all, sober? Hell nah. But I just responded with a polite yes. Then he asked me what day it was. I was excited because I knew the answer this time. "Christmas Eve," I said.

"And if it's 1 am, what day is it?" he inquired further.

Shit. I didn't know what time it was. I didn't know that my freak-out had lasted that long.

"Christmas Day," I said, deflated.

He was happy I knew. He grabbed my feet and another grabbed the upper part of my body, and they loaded me on a stretcher. The ambulance had all its lights flashing in the street. *I hope my neighbors don't see*, I thought. Sure would hate for them to know there's a problem here. Yeah, the daily screaming and trashcan full of bottles doesn't tell them a thing. Sometimes I'm a moron in denial.

We roared off to the hospital where I was transported to a room in the ER to be stitched up. A doctor came in and knew right away he was dealing with an animal. I was covered in bruises. I was underweight. I was lying in a bed with racoon undereye makeup and blood all over my face. As he laced the surgical thread through my mistake, he warned me about the dangers of alcohol and reminded me of the reasons I should be grateful to still be alive.

What a dipshit, dude. Like I don't know the dangers of alcohol? Hello, I had alcohol poisoning when I was 15. I got in wrecks all the time. Sometimes when I drank I ended up doing coke with strangers in another state. Sit down, doc. Let me tell you a tale.

I didn't say much. All the while, a sheriff stood ominously by the door. That was weird. I didn't understand why Johnny Law had to be involved in all this. What I found out later was that when a patient comes in like that, they send you to the nuthouse no matter what. The sheriff is there for those people who feel like they don't want to go. I was much too tired and weak to evade arrest, so I didn't put up a fight.

I was admitted to the mental hospital sometime in the early morning hours of Christmas Day 2007. Happy Holidays, mom and dad! I'm in a lockdown ward.

Coming to the next day was hard. I didn't know where I was. I looked around. There was an empty bed next to me. The room was bare. The sheets and blanket were white. My arm hurt with a burning, swollen pain. And then, I started putting together the shitty timeline. Gah dang! Much to my chagrin, I realized this is the mental hospital and I can't leave! I figured it all out pretty quick, even for my standards.

How in the hell do I get out of here? I cracked the door to my room and waited for someone to start telling me prophesies and theories about the government. It was a little bit of a ghost town, but a few people shuffled through the hallway into the common area. *I have to find an authority figure here, so I can convince them this is all a big misunderstanding.* I began plotting a mission to manipulate just the right people to earn a pass out of this hell-hole. They mandate you see a psychologist, because hello, mental hospital. I waited for my appointment in my room, all alone.

I don't know what happened. I'm pretty sure it was just that my insurance ran out, so after discussing things with the licensed man on campus, they discharged me. I got out with my arm completely wrapped in gauze and blood still on my face from the night before. Before I left, however, they handed me a list of groups in town that might be able to help someone with my particular set of problems. What a bunch of thoughtful and misguided jackasses.

Silver linings are for idealists, and I fancy myself one of those. I figured the silver lining in this experience was that I had finally hit the bottom people talk about. I thought I'd be okay now because if anything is a wake-up call, it's thirteen stitches and a white light experience on the living room floor. But because I have an insane brain when it comes to alcohol, I was just as drunk as I had been when I was admitted within 24 hours.

There was blood on the floor of the dining room when I got home. The knife had gone in the trash. Things looked like a crime scene. Blood spatter wasn't necessary, because I knew things were a mess already. There were a few wonderful things to come of almost dying. I'm not afraid to die now. And just as amazing was the flood that came and swept away a little more of the sand I was trying to stand on to live life. No one wants to stand on something so shaky. Truth be told, I wouldn't have made it long if sand had continued to be my foundation. The cut in my wrist began the deluge that washed all that away. It would take a few more months, but that was the beginning of the end for me. Thank God.

4. JOINING THE CIRCUS

Defeat is a mighty thing. Also, you don't get to pick your roommate.

My last drink was consumed frantically from a Styrofoam cup in the parking lot of the treatment center I was moments away from checking into. Semi-warm domestic beer dribbled down my chin. I hadn't slept well in some time. I looked like a shriveled party lemon on New Year's Day, if that shriveled lemon was a raging alcoholic with unresolved childhood issues.

Rewind maybe three weeks.

I took a trip to the beach in Galveston, Texas as a way to beat the little drinking problem I had acquired. A year before I had gone to the mountains in the same desperate attempt, but managed only to find cocaine and more alcohol. It must have something to do with sea level. It was February, an odd time to be at the beach. Texas weather is equally odd though, so I found it to be pleasant. My husband at the time was pretty resolved to not letting me drink, which would've been a total bummer if I wasn't already used to plowing through everything like a Zamboni to get my way. And this was, after all, a last-ditch effort to solve the problem all by myself like a good, independent person (I wasn't independent in the slightest. Guys, I peed the bed as an adult).

My mind raced upon the minute of my arrival there. *I bet I could drink here. Maybe just one or two. It's the beach! Why wouldn't you drink? You just need a little bit to enjoy yourself.* Anxiety tied me in knots and pushed blood through my veins faster than it should go. I'd have to figure this out. I became a lawyer, even though I only had six college credit hours to my name. And I only had those six college credit hours because I paid a girl in weed to take the online quizzes for me.

I didn't know why, but this old gospel song sung by Hank Williams was playing on repeat in my head: "You're Drifting Too Far From the Shore." Maybe it was just because I was at the beach. Maybe it was because I had made a habit of playing Hank Williams, Bob Dylan, and Woody Guthrie while I was drunk. I would put on their music and lay on the floor next to the speaker with my eyes closed. Then I'd imagine my life wasn't what it was, but instead one where I just happen to be in the studio and decade that these idols had conquered. Whatever the reason, coincidence or Providence, my mind had become a radio.

I jumped at a brief moment of silence to throw out my proposition. *But this time it would be different. This time I would not grow unruly. This time I would behave. I was an alcoholic and I had to drink.* I threw every angle into the fray, trying to get him to acquiesce. If that didn't work, I was prepared to use my sharpened tool of anger. Alcoholism is like that. You don't want to hurt people, but a compulsion far more powerful than any amount of love for another commands you to plow through any obstacle to get the relief you need. It becomes a matter of life and death. This was one such case. (That sounds like the intro to some sick Law & Order episode.)

He finally agreed to split a small amount of alcohol. Beggars can't be choosers, so I took the offer. I finally got enough alcohol to calm the internal and external shaking, then immediately began to wonder how I would get more. This brought on more tension.

I think there are cracks in the universe where just enough light, sanity, love, concern — maybe even God Itself — is allowed to get in from time to time, only when we seem to be ready to receive it. There's maybe a large, cosmos-sized sheet of glass over all the temporal and eternal elements of life. Then, sometimes, when we are at our worst, we happen to be standing underneath a crack in this glass. It's large enough to let in what needs to be let in, but still too small to see. Through this sliver, the glitter of stars and the warmth of everything good can sprinkle down on us — heal, soothe, reassure, satisfy, and move us to take one way or the other. This theory is probably all bullshit, but if it were provable, the world might have seen one of these cracks right above my head in Galveston, Texas that February night in 2008.

I began to think about my life — where I had been and where I was going. The proverbial writing was splattered all over the wall. I knew, conceded, and finally could not escape the reality that I was dying. I would be dead within the year if I kept on. I knew that. I was 22-years-old.

I don't know why this revelation came so suddenly. It had been true the day before, the week before, the year before. Somehow, I had been able to evade the truth, but not anymore. I came to a clearing in the woods. I saw myself lonely, beat up, defeated. I realized my life was no longer my own, that I had been overrun by some mad train engineer hellbent on careening down the tracks at dangerous speeds until my engine finally collided with a wall. The engineer might live on, but I wouldn't. I knew then that I was powerless. There was no longer a choice in drinking. It had become, so quietly and surely, something I had to do no matter what.

Alcoholism had never and would never ask my opinion about anything. Even if I didn't want to, I was going to drink. Even if I was on probation and faced jail time if caught, I was going to drink. Even if I knew it would one day kill me, I was going to drink.

With what little energy I had left, I threw a little shredded white flag into the clearing surrounded by scary ghosts and ominous warnings. I gave up.

The little motel I was staying in was right across the street from the lapping waves of the Gulf of Mexico. Ocean water sounded like a great altar, plus I was buzzed and motel carpet didn't sound good enough for such a declaration. I walked across the street and down the narrow concrete steps that led to the sand. It was cool beneath my feet. I watched the waves hug the shore, then retreat back to their mother. The blanket of darkness above me was studded with tiny pinpricks of twinkling light. If there was a God, maybe It would hear me here.

Then, something very peculiar happened. A voice – some inner, small voice – spoke to me and said, "You should get on your knees." Hearing voices isn't always the best thing, you know? What's worse is when you answer it. "I'm not getting on my knees. That's what weird, spiritual people do," I responded. And as suddenly as it had come, the voice spoke again, "Right now, I don't think it really matters." That was convincing enough and I landed knee first in a pile of smoldering destruction in front of the dark water and night sky.

"God, if you give a shit, I'm in a mess and I need some help. I can't get myself out of it."

This was what I remember of the prayer I prayed to a God I wasn't sure existed. If one did, It certainly didn't care about me. That's what I thought.

I drank the next morning and every day that followed until I wound up in the parking lot of the treatment center. Sometime around 4 o'clock on March 6, 2008 is when I left a dying circus to join a new one. I walked into the place and it smelled like Band-Aids. An older blonde woman they called Linda greeted me. She looked at me standing there all spun around, mixed up, drunk but not violent yet, lost, chained to a self-created prison. She wrapped me in warm arms, oozing genuine love and concern even though she didn't know me at all, and said, "I am so glad to see you." It's enough to make a drunk cry, really. Then again, drunks cry at almost anything I guess. Must be all the wine and maudlin self-pity.

The next morning, I woke up in a hospital bed to the smell of eggs. Worst case scenario for someone nursing an 8-year hangover. I slid out of bed and set my feet on a cold linoleum floor. Today, I was to meet the others in the circus. The first was a young heroin addict. They told me he was going to show me around the grounds – where we ate, where we smoked, where we huddled in a circle to talk about our god damn feelings. I followed him around, limping as fast I could to keep up. Before checking in, my foot went head to head with a wall in my house, and my destruction was only stopped on account of the fact that walls sometimes have studs in them to keep them intact. I'm pretty sure I broke my toe that day, but I never saw a doctor about it.

There was a girl in the "Butt Hut," our designated smoking area, who for the sake of this writing I'll call "Brianna." She was without a doubt the meanest girl there. She scared the shit out of me, but I guess that wasn't hard on my first day sober. I think she even scared the guys. She ran methamphetamine between Waco and Fort Worth before getting there. *Please don't be my roommate, please don't be my roommate, please Jesus, don't let her be my roommate,* I thought. When I was finally walked into my room, staring right back at me was Brianna, pretty pissed that she was going to have to share a living space. After several nights of me lying as still as possible, we struck up a conversation. She liked frogs a lot. She had grown up with money. She was, I learned, as scared and lost as I was.

I spent exactly thirty days there. I learned what illness I had and how to treat it. When I got out, I found more clowns who had the same condition. We hung out, drank coffee, smoked too many cigarettes, and said "fuck" and "God" in the same sentence. A lonely person like me, someone who had hid myself away as much as possible for the safety of others, was now a member of a strange tribe. Together, we were – we are – a legion of odd fellows, outcast pirates, liars, thieves. We have sailed with tempests, but gave up our sinking vessels for new lifeboats. And we don't steal anymore, and we try not to lie so much. Each day, I get to meet girls like me, and I do my best to help them in the same ways people helped me. For all its idiosyncrasies, it's a fun circus to be a part of.

And that, boys and girls, is the story of how I ran off to join the circus completely sober – not like that time I tripped acid in 2002 and sincerely thought the carnival was a viable option.

5. COMING BY WAY OF KNOCK-OUT

All of Life's crap is great because it makes the good stuff really, really good.

One time I was handcuffed in the back of a squad car in front of my house, my second arrest. I felt like the arresting officer was being a real asshole. I didn't really care that my mom and ex-husband, whom I had hurt and worried very badly, were watching me be hauled off yet again from the safety of the front porch. I was wholly consumed with myself in every way. I was of no real use to anyone, couldn't take care of myself, and I rested like a lead weight on the shoulders of everyone who was unfortunate enough to be in my life.

I was violent. I was miserable. I was drowning in a river I created with anger, resentment, and selfishness.

But one day all that changed. Coming by way of knockout... Uh, I mean a mental health ward (!!!), I met some real nice people who once felt like I did. I found a new way to live. I let go, rushed downstream, and found myself in the flow. Groovy, dude. It's a real thing.

The darkness of my life is what has made the light so much brighter. Today, I gathered with those nice people again and we laughed and we remembered the times we were so sad and lost. We laughed at our old misfortunes, having been plucked from the pile of sorrowful human bullshit and placed neatly on dry ground by none other than God Himself.

I also marched with a student of mine and some other friends. My feet got dirty, and I didn't care. I am

29

among the living. Count me in.

All this joy – this flow of light, love, and life – is set against my backdrop of hospital trips, lockdown wards, broken relationships, pain, treatment centers, hopelessness, wreckage and selfish misery. When I realize what my life is today, I'm so happy I could cry. And I do. It happens in my car when I'm driving from one place to another. It happens when I talk to girls like me, who are unsure of what life in recovery might feel like.

Good God, I am alive. I'm here.

I remember the time I was lost. I love that I am found.

II.

NOT IMMACULATE
CONCEPTION

6. RUN THE LIGHT, MOM! I'M HAVING A BABY!

It took forty-five hours to grow up.

My sister, my mom, and I had spent the evening packing boxes for troops. I was neck deep in beef jerky, Crystal Light packets, and playing cards. Story of my life, right? I left the ladies to finish the work and went home to go to sleep. It had been a long day. I crawled all 180 pounds of my 9-month pregnant body into a very cozy bed and fell asleep...for about two hours.

Something was burning in my back. It was a waving ache, vibrating out from my spine. It woke me up, but I figured it was from all the work I'd done that day and didn't immediately freak out. I tried rearranging my body, hugging the stupid pillow that helped me feel less like a loner. That dumbass pillow never even took me out to eat or told me I looked nice. It's OK though. I burned it after I gave birth.

The ache didn't go away and I decided to call my labor coach — my experienced, trusty, ever faithful Mom. She knocked at the door ten minutes later. We strolled a few times around the block under the November moon. I was smiling, excited that it looked like the page was turning after being stuck on the same uncomfortable chapter for nine months. When we felt like the contractions were coming at regular intervals, we calmly got into the car and headed for Providence Hospital.

The nurse on duty hooked me up to all kinds of fancy robots. I heard Ava's heartbeat, her kicks, her

32

cramped movement inside my belly. Oh, what a miracle! How lovely! How nice! After the standard hour of monitoring, the nurse came in with a pleasant smile and proceeded to violate me in the way pregnant women become accustomed to. What's this? My cervix isn't dilating? I told the nurse the contractions were uncomfortable. She informed me Medicaid — the only insurance I had — wouldn't pay for anything unless I was in "active labor", which is determined by cervix dilation. Since I wasn't in what the State would define as active labor, I couldn't be admitted. They gave me a sleeping pill to take home with me. Disappointed, I left the hospital.

The contractions kept me from sleeping any, but I didn't take the pill. And they got worse. By 6 am I wasn't smiling; by noon I was crying; by nightfall I was looking for a gun. The pain moved from the back to the front — clench, squeeze, and release. The twisted muscle tango that women are cursed with during labor rolled in like a storm a sailor sees from the deck of his ship. The waves were getting wilder, and I couldn't seem to find a life jacket anywhere.

I rocked the assault on my muscles for that whole day and into the night. I was so tired, but I couldn't sleep. I finally broke and decided to take the pill that nice nurse had given me.

It was Ambien for Christ's sake. Sure, I had been up for more than forty-eight hours at that point, not including the small nap I had taken before my contractions started. And yeah, I could've used some sleep. But instead of sleeping I went shopping with my second-string labor coach, a girl named Summer Shine (seriously, that's her name). Apparently, I had become too much for my mom to handle. The cussing had intensified with the contractions. I was a wild animal, rolling like a crazy person on an exercise ball because I had seen it on that show *A Baby Story* a gazillion times. And for the record, that shit doesn't work. Nothing works. What are those hippies thinking? You're just going to roll your fat ass around on a stability ball and your baby will feel the vibe and come on down because the price is right? Idiots. All of them.

Summer followed behind me while I moaned like some pioneer woman in the middle of a Walmart on Franklin Avenue. It was the only place open at 2 am and we seized the opportunity to get out of the house. I didn't realize it until after I came home from the hospital, but I bought fuzzy pink socks made especially for diabetics, back pain patches, and candy. When a contraction would hit, I'd lean over the cart and Summer would rub my back. If I knew how bad we were freaking out the stockers, I would have given them a better show. Unfortunately, pain superseded my usual knack for performance. Summer told me later she assumed everyone thought we were a lesbian couple about to welcome their first child. I didn't even have a chance to get into character. Damn you, labor pains.

Feeling like an amputee patient on a civil war battlefield, I told my mom we should go back to the hospital. Again with the fancy machinery and standard violation. And again, no change in dilation. This time, however, the nurses informed me I couldn't scream and drop F-bombs in the labor and delivery wing because women were "trying to have their babies." Perhaps it was the lack of sleep, or maybe it was that a 7-pound human being that was trying to get out of my body, but I had forgotten I lived in America and not some Nordic village where bellowing out the pains of hell is widely accepted as normal practice.

I huffed to the nurse in between the tremors, "If you expect me to come here tomorrow morning to be induced, you better give me something strong RIGHT NOW. Something even John Belushi would get excited about. Don't send me away without some kind of relief, or you're going to burn in hell for all eternity. I WILL WRITE A LETTER TO YOUR BOSS, lady!" She came back after a phone call with my doctor. In her hand was a syringe filled with chemical relief.

"What…is…it?" I asked.

"Stadol," she said. "It's high-powered and it should work. It's also the only thing we can give you."

And bam, into my hip the needle went. After a few seconds, I was granted some mercy. Whew! I had never welcomed a needle so much in my life!

The old man who greets people at the front door, the one I had nearly set ablaze with my wild eyes when walking in 45 minutes prior, was still sitting in the same spot. I waved and cracked a joke as I exited the hospital. It's smooth sailing now, brother. I hadn't eaten this entire time so my mom drove me out to Luby's. I rode shotgun, thanking God for science, and thanking science for Stadol.

When we got about a mile away from the world's greatest cafeteria restaurant, the pain came rushing back with a vengeance — WORSE THAN EVER. Was this some kind of trick to get me to leave the hospital quietly? Oh, I'm writing that letter now. Plans changed and we got the food togo. At home I crawled into the bed, wailing at the ceiling, eyes clenched shut. My mom spoon fed me a few bites of food. *THIS IS BULLSHIT.* My champion called the nurses back. "She's worse than before. How long was this stuff supposed to last?" I got up from the bed and BOOM. It felt like my water broke. What I know now that I didn't know then was about twenty minutes after that nurse's thumb left the button on the syringe, I went into active labor. Medicine: a cruel joke.

Positive that a baby was about to exit my person, I screamed with the force of Satan himself, "Get in the car NOW!!" I hobbled to the passenger seat; Mom was at the wheel. Zoom, zoom, zoom down Sanger Avenue to what I felt like was going to be the shores of Omaha Beach. Oh God, a yellow light ahead. "Run it, mom!!!"

She didn't. She didn't run the light! They run the lights in the movies, Mom!! God Almighty! So help me God, I will cut every last one of you if I don't get to the hospital right now!

The old man at the door made the sign of the cross as I got onto the elevator. I gave him a good, ol' fashioned middle finger salute. We made it back to the hospital bed I had laid in twice in the last two days. The nurses looked at me.

Oh God, she's back.

The one gentle, tolerant nurse I had come to like told me she wouldn't make me wait the hour you're supposed to. She said she'd come back in thirty minutes to check me for dilation. It was the longest thirty minutes of my life. I gripped the bed's railing when the waves of pain would crash on my body's hull. Some girl who had been in labor for two seconds, still wearing her maternity skirt and PEARLS, was in the bed next to me. I must have sounded like a sick cow right before you nail it between the eyes with a bullet. She, on the other hand, didn't make a peep and somehow got admitted before me. What a polite bitch.

After the allotted time had passed, the nurse returned. I welcomed the violation. Had I gone from 3 centimeters to 4? Was I going to have to go home again without any hope? Was I going to have to do this for even one more hour?

No. My cervix had dilated to 4 centimeters. The State would be satisfied and the hospital could treat me. The anesthesiologist/nicest man on the planet came into the fancy room they had assigned me to give me my epidural. He made small talk which was total bullshit, but I appeased him as best I could because he was the man with the needle.

"Yes…OHHHH…the weather…OWWWWW… is rather mild for November."

As the medicine joined my blood in the race through my veins, numbness came over all the painful parts and I breathed a sigh of real relief for the first time in over 36 hours. And then I finally fell asleep.

At approximately 8:30-8:45 pm, I woke up feeling

lots of pressure in the, um, exit area. Summer got the nurse. I was ready to push.

If you've never had your feet in stirrups with your very private nether regions exposed for all of God and country to see, *and* at the same time not cared a single bit, then you really haven't lived. So, there I was, hoisted up like some barn animal, surrounded by my mom, Debbie Sims, Summer, my sister Faith, the backup doctor and a nurse. "Push!" they said. I focused very hard on doing everything right. Determined to grow up finally, I bared down with what little strength I had left. I did the work millions of women before me had done with a cemented sense of purpose.

At 9:30 pm, November 19th, 2009, a Thursday, Ava Lorene emerged from my body — calm, serene and on her own time. At 9:30 pm, November 19th, 2009, a Thursday, I was honorably admitted to a league of extraordinary women. We both had crossed a threshold, and both of us were new.

Ava didn't make a sound until the nurse started cleaning her up. I saw a spot on her hand and asked a series of nervous questions: "What is that? Is she ok? Does she have two eyes and ten toes?" When I was pregnant, I had a dream Ava had thirteen toes on one foot and five eyes on her forehead, so this question was very relevant. Lobster hands were also a big concern for me. Happily, Ava was perfectly fine. And so was I.

From my bed I heard her let out a little cry, the kind babies make in the movies. As I heard my daughter make her first audible impression on this world, I laid my head on the pillow, shut my eyes, and knew this race was over. Finally.

Ava continues to operate on her own schedule and I've continued to tell her, "Hurry!" She taught me patience during that forty-five hours, and has continued to do so every day for the last eight years.

I don't know why things happen the way they do. I don't know why Life doesn't abide by the script I wrote when I was younger. But I do know that I have this story now. It's not the one I would have written if I had control of the pen, but it's better this way. I'm the protagonist in my life, not exactly the author. Don't even get me started on the battle between agency and fatalism. Let's get coffee sometime and talk about it. Despite the challenges, I've been given the best co-star a mother could ever ask for. The narrative seems to be progressing nicely – plenty of conflict. And at the very least, it keeps me busy.

7. AN EDICT FROM THE LEAGUE OF EXTRAORDIANRY WOMEN

Okay, okay, okay. I wrote it in anger.

From the minutes taken at a meeting of the League of Extraordinary Women:

Through a series of very predictable and scientifically explained events, a woman found herself in the Court of Noble Bitches, frustrated and bitter. She approached the oak podium, weighted with the burden of a thousand idiots, and breathed a heavy sigh into the microphone. Her words, soaked with bewilderment and dissatisfaction, rolled off her stained lips and into the pierced ears of the bold women who had come before her. After several minutes, the court issued this decree:

"Fathers, a term which we define as those endowed with the physical capacity to procreate (however mistakenly), to be always and forever known as different from the concept of being a Daddy, must get with the [expletive redacted] program.

In some cases, the result of the five clumsy minutes of natural human behavior is much costlier in time, money, and emotion than originally anticipated. But so be it. It is hereby ordered that you grow a pair, pay what is due, or get out of the way.

From henceforth members of this League will take lessons learned and operate accordingly, using discernment and tact most of the time, and vicious sarcasm when necessary. Not absolved of responsibility, the women of this League acknowledge and own their mistakes and encourage fathers, as understood by the previous definition, to do the same. Learn how to not be a dick, or get the [expletive redacted] out of here. Godspeed and Good Luck."

8. PARENTING: OMG LET'S PANIC

Don't worry. You won't screw your kids up as bad as you think you will.

Since I'm in the poor man's business of giving opinions, here's one I like to hand out to struggling moms.

I used to think the goals of all parents, big and small, were just a derivative of a singular goal – which is to not screw their children up as much as their parents screwed them up. Family business is tough.

But the reality is you're going to screw your kids up in an entirely new way. Make it fun! Make it exciting! But keep the damage to a minimum. Therapy can get expensive.

I used to blame my parents for all my peculiar emotional twists. "If Dad had said 'I love you' more…" "If mom had asked me what went wrong at school instead of kicking me out of the suburban at soccer practice…." Nick-At-Night and its repetitious playing of *Leave It to Beaver* was also a killer. And I didn't even watch *Leave It to Beaver*. I just heard through the therapy circuit that it screws a lot of people up.

I suppose it's the Universe's cruel joke, but I didn't realize my parents were human until I became a parent myself. And after living on the planet for a while, I guess I've come to understand that most people are just doing the best they can with what they have to work with. I was an incredibly selfish teenager, and I didn't know how to appreciate dysfunction. Their vindication came with a letter I wrote a week before graduating college. I told them they did well in "raising a child in the way they should go." The drama-queen-prodigal-daughter had finally come home, waving her apologetic banner like a distress signal: "You were right!"

So now I have a kid of my own – a four-year-old if you want to get specific about it. She's in the defiance stage, and I've found myself in the muddy, crayon-filled trenches of parenthood, trying my best to teach her principles. This is what gratitude is; this is what selfishness and unselfishness are; you better eat that oatmeal I made or all hell is going to break loose.

And man, she's not having it. As the mother of the house, I feel like what I say should be treated like gospel. I am the law. I am the supreme ruler. And I'm just a tad bit self-righteous.

With each step on the path of motherhood, I've learned more and more that I have no clue what I'm doing. That's scary to admit on a public forum, but it's true. When Ava was small, it was easy to do lots of things right. I fed her, I changed her, I bathed her, and I put her to sleep. End of story.

But as she's grown older and learned she has a mind of her own, and that other people are on the planet besides me and the rest of her family, it's become a lot harder to raise her. And in those books I've skimmed over the years, I don't hear a lot of them talk about being human – the idea that you're going to try and fail. A lot.

Like any spiritually inclined person, I decided to talk to Ava about the concept of God. It's no secret that a spiritual way of life was lost on me for well over a decade.

But now I say prayers. I do that. It helps. Anyway, I tried to introduce Ava to that practice. She's been getting in trouble at school for her behavior and suggested we say a prayer about that.

In a sweet, motherly voice: "Sometimes mommy doesn't know how to behave, so I ask for help with that. You can, too."

"I don't want to pray, mama!"

Oh God. I'm raising a heathen. My tone grew frustrated. "Well, it's just an idea. It helps. And if you get in trouble again at school today then you're not watching a movie tonight and THERE WILL BE NO HOT CHOCOLATE," I said. This was met by a loud whine – the kind that makes you want to stick your fingers in your ears and scream louder than the kid doing the whining.

My thoughts as I grimaced: *For God's sake, Ava. You have a bed to sleep in, you have food to eat, and you have clothes to wear! Life is not that bad! Some people have it much worse! There are women right now who are hitting a crack pipe, yelling at their kids to get away from the bathroom door!*

But she doesn't know this. And I realized yet again that it's my job to teach her. I am, after all, the supreme ruler. (I'm perhaps under-qualified for this position.)

This particular day, instead of being a perfect example of a mother, I turned into a four-year-old myself. After my dramatic explanation of life that was barely intelligible through my muttering, I got hit with a humbling epiphany. The words I had uttered minutes before about prayer and behavior punched me square in the chest. "Mommy

44

doesn't know how to behave sometimes and she needs help with that."

Guess what, guys. Mommy doesn't know how to be a mommy sometimes.

That whole cliché about there being no manual is a real thing. Plenty of authors with degrees from highly esteemed universities have made millions off trying to sell flailing parents the answers. But the truth is there isn't one single formula for how to do this incredibly daunting task of raising a child in the way they should go. It's not a paint-by-numbers. It's a mix of happiness and frustration, and you just do your best and hope they don't grow up to be a murderer.

All of this isn't to say I'm a complete moron with no clue how to perform basic tasks. I'm a smart girl, and don't you forget it. But I'm also as human as I've ever been. For me, and this is just for me, parenting is a series of tempered freak-outs. Each day is a new mission, and each night is a time to reflect on what I've learned by trying to teach, and what I've realized I'm still not perfect at. This is one of the rewards of parenting for me. It's the reminder that I'm a human being on the planet and so is Ava. In our own way, we're growing up together.

June Cleaver was a character made up by a team of writers to sell dish soap and household appliances during a time of economic prosperity. She never really raised those damn kids. Susan Duty is a real 28-year-old woman, fallible in her own right, who was assigned the very real job of mothering Ava.

There are no commercial breaks, no second takes, and

45

no advertising revenue.

They say motherhood is the hardest job you'll ever love, and that's true. It has a wealth of rewards that can't be obtained through any other means. But instilling morals and principles in a child that is a grueling task, especially at an age when they're the center of their own universe.

The grand ol' irony of the whole thing is I'm still learning a lot of these lessons myself. I guess I'll always be learning them.

I used to think I had to have all the answers. I guess I should help Dr. So-And-So-Who-Probably-Doesn't-Even-Have-Kids pay for their condo in Boca Raton and buy one of those fancy parenting books. Whatever.

My parents did a good job of giving me the tools I need to survive here. In the process of transferring said tools, I wrote them off as total idiots. In the time between then and now, Life has served me up a hearty piece of humble pie. I'll never be able to accurately express how much I love them for exactly who they are – strengths, faults and all.

I have one wish and one demand. My wish is that these principles I'm trying to instill in Ava cement themselves in her little soul somewhere. My demand is that when Ava inevitably comes running back home like the prodigal daughter, she does more than wave a banner. I expect fireworks and a hug.

9. SCOTTISH TIGER WARRIOR PRINCESS

Parenting is being slowly choked by someone who continues to demand more and more money from you until you die.

Strong, heavy, formidable metal – a moving, wheeled fortress. The B52 Bomber of bicycles. Black like a military-grade weapon with neon pink lettering. This is Ava's new bike, the one that's just a little too big for her.

Learning to ride this gargantuan monster was going to be a mighty assignment. We went to the park where a field of grass seemed the safest spot to practice the art of crashing. I'm an early 90s kid, the second in a litter of 5. We crashed on pavement without helmets because Mom was too busy chasing the others to give us ominous warnings about the dangers of riding without protection. When the brakes failed, instincts and self-preservation kicked in and told us to wipe out in the neighbor's yard. We were alright. Bill Clinton was president. Neon was in. Wind suits could be torn and it wasn't the end of the world.

But now, I'm a mother myself and we live in a dangerous world. Donald Trump will soon dictate foreign policy from his Twitter account while he takes a shit in the morning. Wind suits are dead. There is no helmet for this.

We walked the bike about half a mile to the park. Ava ascended her metal steed, uneasy. "I won't let go, Ava," I assured her. Away we bounced over the dips and earthy raises in the open space of the park. Tipping and leaning, wheeling and reeling. We were living full-contact life this day. But as it does, fear showed up to crash the party.

"I can't do this!" Ava yelled. Little seven-year-old tears collected in the corners of her eyes among the blonde eyelashes God gave her. I stopped. She sat on the ground with more reasons for her decision to quit.

In so many ways, I saw myself sitting in her shadow. I looked at her red bangs and saw Susan Duty, as a child and even now, overcome with cold fear about the tasks ahead of me. I didn't want her to grow up with the same perspective of fear I had when I was her age. I decided to tell her what I know now, and maybe that's what parenting is.

"Ava," I said with the authority of a mother who has a lesson to share. "Do you want to know something?" She looked up, as if to say "of course! Help me!"

"You're already the bravest girl in the world. Everything you need to conquer every scary thing in the world is already in you; you just have to unlock it."

I started to realize what I was saying.

"You have Scottish ancestry. Your great great-great-great-great-great Grandmas and Grandpas looked invaders right in the eye and didn't even care. They were bona fide nuts in some respects, and because they were fearless, they were free. Everything you have to be fearless is already there. You're a tiger. You're a fighter! You're tough and smart! You can do this!"

She rose from the soil ready to try again, and we rolled around for another 15 minutes or so. I never let go, because I accepted that today the lesson wasn't how to ride a bike without training wheels. It was about something else. We ditched her new wheels to go play at the playground nearby. After hide-and-seek, a swing or two, and a visit to the trees in the distance, we decided to return home.

On a whim, I decided to carry her on my back while I rode the bike home. Sure, it looked ridiculous, but when was the last time I gave a shit about that? Today, I realized I am a Scottish Warrior Tiger Princess, and I gave birth to one, too. We are powerful beings, gifted by God with resilience, wit, and a big dose of Go-Get-'Em.

Ava clung to my back like a baby koala. It was fantastic, until I realized she had to hold onto my throat to stay upright. And parenting is just like that I suppose. It's magnificent, realizing truth in a field. And then sometimes it's a small human clinging to you, slowly choking the last bit of life out of you as you try to just get home.

It's an adventure that any tiger can handle, at least with a little help.

10. DON'T DROWN

Sometimes you have to almost die to remember to live.

This is what happened when I almost drowned 8 days before my 30th birthday.

A flash of neon pink streaked across the sky. Ava was coming into the water off her raft in the deepest part of the wave pool. The waves were rolling at least four feet above my head. I saw her face, her neon bathing suit and the clear, blue, plastic tube. I had just enough time to think *oh shit*, and knew immediately we were in a lot of trouble.

My brain instantaneously came up with a plan: get to the side where I saw the ladder. I lifted Ava above my head as high as I could. The waves rolled easily over us. I hustled through the water as fast as I could, desperately gasping for air, but only getting sprays of water in my mouth and nose.

When I reached something to grab, I planted my hand and clamped my fingers as tightly as I could to the ladder cut into the concrete of the pool. Another wave came, knocking me loose. I fought for my place again. I gripped for life, but the next wave moved me like I was holding nothing at all. I lifted Ava up higher. She suddenly felt heavier and I looked up to make sure she was alive. I didn't know how much water was getting in her mouth.

I yelled, "STOP!"

Nothing stopped. Another wave came and inundated us with more water. No air. I kept holding Ava up, all forty pounds of her, as high as I could. In my head I thought,

Get her out of the pool. I reached again for the ladder, and I yelled again. Nothing changed. The waves were still coming, I still wasn't getting air and Ava was swallowing water, too. I knew if the waves kept coming for much longer, they were going to supersede my strength to fight. I couldn't breathe. I wanted so desperately for someone to save my Ava.

I came right up to the edge of total desperation when I finally heard a long, sustained whistle. I came back to reality. There was suddenly air to breathe and the tight pains in my chest from holding my breath and panicking went away. As quickly as they started, the waves stopped. I looked up, thinking the life guard would be above me. A woman swam to me, also frantic. I don't remember what she said. I heard someone from behind me ask, "Are you okay?" It was a young, blonde lifeguard. She extended her red raft to Ava and helped her get a hold of it. With a disgusted, vicious look on my face I responded to what I felt was a wholly asinine question. "No, I am not fucking okay," I snarled.

Suddenly I could stand with my head above the water. I looked over to see my husband, who didn't know anything was wrong, floating among the onlookers. Everyone was staring. "Can you get off your fucking raft?!" I screamed. We didn't say thank you to the lifeguard. I took Ava by the hand, shaking, and walked her out of the water and away from the scene without saying anything else. And that was it.

Adrenaline was still raging in my veins, but we were out of danger. I started crying uncontrollably, and I cried for the next two hours. When it stopped, I was silent and stoic. I didn't feel much of anything.

Yard work needed to be done. I was outside looking at the lawn mower when the neighbor came up and made small talk with Clint. The neighbor talked about Saint Augustine grass. I always just figured I was the kind of person that on days I nearly lost my life, I'd be able to tell the neighbor something like, "Who gives a fuck about Saint Augustine grass, man? What are we even doing here?" But I didn't do that. I stood there and listened to him politely. I guess grass matters sometimes to some people, and that's okay.

I sifted through all the falling stars of thought that sprinkled the expanse of my fuzzy, dreamy consciousness. It was so much, but one thread ran throughout, thicker than any other thought. When I shut my eyes, one thing lit up the black between my eye lids and my mind...

My little Ava.

As a baby. As a little girl. In the backseat of the car. Taking a walk down the street when she was a toddler. Taking a nap in a bucket when I managed at Poppa Rollo's Pizza. What she looked like the times I woke her up as an infant. Staring at her in a rocking chair during a 2am feeding. I juxtaposed all these warm thoughts against the knowledge of myself. How irresponsible I am. How dumb I have been in my life. How selfishly I've lived for so long. I let tears run down my face.

My time to uphold that heavy responsibility of being a mother came some years ago. It was a little serendipity, a little absentmindedness. I was to grow this human inside my body. I didn't plan it. I didn't ask for it. It happened. I had no idea you could love someone else so much.

I thought about what it was like when she was a baby and I had a minimum wage job. I used to ask her dad for help with diapers and formula. He always told me the same thing: that he couldn't help now, but he would when he was able. I brought the diapers home from the store and I was proud of myself.

I remember holding her above the water as high as I could. I was scared it wasn't high enough and that water was taking her over as much as it was me.

My mom told me I was the Mama Bear. I did my job. God, I didn't know. I didn't know your heart and soul could walk around like that. I didn't know my heart and soul had blue eyes and red hair. I wonder what the fifteen-year-old me would say about having a daughter like Ava. I wonder if younger Susan would have laughed or gotten excited. I wonder if I would have ever believed life was like this when I was so young.

I knew if Ava got out of the pool I would be okay. I did the best I could. I've always been doing the best I could. I can't help but weep to think of how lucky I am to have been given the job.

I held her that night, as overtaken with the love I have for her and my life as a mom as I had been with other things earlier. There's a lot of shit that matters, and there's even more shit that doesn't. I don't know when I'm leaving here. My skin and bones are a rental. But when I do go, I want to leave behind something beautiful. I want to leave the world better than how I found it. I think God did the job for me when He gave me Ava. And to think, I never saw it coming.

Didn't see the wave either.

11. MOTHER'S DAY

Mother's Day is the one day a year you get to take a nap and not feel guilty about it.

I am mother to the one, Ava. Maybe you've heard of her. She's a fire breathing dragon with grit and Scottish ancestry. She made me a mom 7 years ago. She's the reason I get taken to lunch once a year, usually by my own mother, and celebrated for getting thrown up on more than a human should. I wasn't ready for her, but life has a funny way of not really giving a shit about that.

She came into the world peaceful and quiet. It wasn't until they started messing with her that she cried for the first time. This was, of course, after 45 hours of labor – which according to the universal mother bylaws I am entitled to mention each and every time I discuss her birth. It was 45 hours, dude. I had my first real whip of motherly fear when I realized she was outside the womb finally and I didn't have her in my hands. We learned together how to trust God, to chill out and wait on the "It's ok" to settle in.

Ava is the one who got me back into college. I looked at her in her little makeshift, janky Rollo's playpen and realized I had to make something of myself. If it hadn't been for her, maybe I would have never darkened the doors of Baylor University. Maybe I would have kept on the way of mediocrity. Those nights reading textbooks to her while I laid on the floor next to her crib were hard, but I know those moments went straight to the highlight reel.

She'll be in second grade next year. Somehow, she and I have become our own little team. We're travel buddies. We jet set. We eat brownies for breakfast in

Manhattan at Christmas time. In ten months, we'll watch the sun go down over the Pacific Ocean. We've come a long way from Ramen and heartbreak. Take that, adversity!

She still gets me up every morning. I told her today on the way to school that we'll be where we're at now for a while longer, so that mommy can be a writer. I said one day we'll have our own house, and maybe it'll even have stairs. Ava wants a house with stairs for some reason.

For Mother's Day, I just want to take a nap and have Ava give me a hug. She has given me more than she knows already.

12. WHAT WAS ASSAD LIKE IN FIRST GRADE?

Dictators and terrorists were six years old once.

Peace is made at home. War isn't a problem for the cosmos to solve.

A conversation with my daughter, age 7. She began:

"Let me tell you about Drake. He is MEAN. Today, I didn't do nothin' to him and when I was sitting down on the rug, criss-cross applesauce, he looked at me and said, 'Ha, ha, you were the last one to the rug.'"

I responded with what I thought was profound insight. "Do you think Drake gets his feelings hurt? Sometimes people respond with anger when they're scared."

"He ain't scared of nothin'," she said.

And then I realized I'm raising a future Supreme Court justice, or a president, or a congresswoman, or a Teach for America candidate. I wonder who imparted life lessons to Assad. I wonder what fear he must have when he lays his head down on his down pillow at night.

I wonder if idealism should be abandoned and if I should just start telling Ava the capabilities of Tomahawk missiles.

No, I shouldn't. As for me and my house, we will put our banners in cement that goes ten feet deep. We'll hold fast to the idea that peace is first a local concern. She and I are pebbles thrown into the ocean. What we do here goes out there.

Lessons in diplomacy and humanitarianism don't begin in political science courses, Washington D.C. or when you get your 501c3. They begin at the dinner table.

They are now. They aren't later.

Parenting is spiritual work.

13. AT THE CORNER OF CAVITY AND NOW

For best results, do scary things as often as possible. Repeat as necessary.

The dentist's office was filled with nervous, excited kids this morning. Ava sat in her chair, mesmerized at the paintings on the wall and kid-friendly iPads they had for them to use. She wouldn't mind coming back here. In the months leading up to this appointment, I used fear to convince her to brush her teeth so cavities wouldn't erode her chompers. Any anxiety she had sitting in this office was my fault and I accepted it.

At 6:30 this morning, I was searching for screenwriting events in the L.A. area for the weekend I will be visiting. I figured since I was going to be there anyway, I might as well see if there's some kind of opportunity for me to take advantage of – one where I can blend in inconspicuously, for the sole purpose of learning. The only thing I found was a Scriptwriter's Network social. A SOCIAL. Literally the worse imaginable scenario for me.

I'm an introvert who appears extroverted. I don't like going to parties, and my idea of a great Friday night is sitting at home in absolute silence. If I get crazy, maybe I'll watch a documentary and drink Diet Dr. Pepper. I'm fine with this lifestyle. It's safe and comfortable for me.

So, when I saw this party for screenwriter's happening the same night I was to arrive in L.A., my first reaction was to pull my hand back from what appeared to be a fire. What would I do? Sit in the corner and drink

Diet Dr. Pepper while I avoid conversation with men I just automatically judge as pervy weirdos? Maybe I could sit there and compare myself to everyone in the room, because OMG THAT SOUNDS LIKE FUN. Maybe I could just go in there and make a few jokes, start to feel awkward, then walk out and wonder if I remembered where I parked my rental car in this strange ass town. Fear strikes again!

Ava was brought back to the room painted with little tooth fairies. She sat in a purple dentist's chair and let the nice assistant clean her mouth. She opened wide and only squirmed a little. I kept telling her she was doing great. The lady advised her to pay special attention to her gums when she brushes and congratulated her for not having any cavities. That was a relief to me, because Lord knows I thought maybe her mouth was full of them.

As I watched Ava be a seven-year-old warrior, my eyes started to mist. I had one of those moments I have sometimes when I remember a time before she could talk, when she was in diapers, or when she started to take her first steps. I couldn't believe she was in second grade and that we had made it this far. I was also worried that she was scared as she sat in that chair and wasn't showing it. That's a feeling you have when you have kids. It's this feeling of your spirit being connected with something outside yourself. To make it worse, you can't really control that outside part. Well, shit.

I know I want Ava to grow up to be brave. She should have the courage of Wonder Woman. She'll need it in a world like this. To foster this attitude, I should tell her she is brave when she is – for example, in this purple dentist's chair that she was petrified of until she realized it wasn't really that bad. I should also walk my own talk. I should go to that party at a bar on Wilshire Boulevard in Los Angeles, California on September 1st. I should talk to other people, because that's what's scary. When chasing down something impossible, you must do scary things often.

Ava and I are powerful women who come across dragons and evil villains all the time. We learn together every day. She won't realize it until she's in her 30s, but she teaches me as much as I try to teach her. That's something we can all drink to.

14. GRATEFUL

Gratitude makes what you have enough. and it feels better than drugs most of the time.

She told me tonight as I cuddled in bed with her that she'd love me forever and ever and ever and ever and ever (plus 25 more "evers"). My eyes grew glossy on the fifteenth "ever", and by the time she was done, I felt that feeling I sometimes get bubble up just below my sternum.

I think about a lot of things. Strange things. I cry more than most people. Tonight, little, wet drops of happy memories slipped down my cheeks as I thought of how lucky I am to have been given the charge of raising a redhead like Ava. One of the thoughts that rolled through my head was: I don't ever want to die so that I don't ever have to leave Ava here alone. Then I remembered I would. Then I remembered it's ok. It has always been ok. Always. Sometimes "OK" looks like a disaster. And that is, you guessed it... just fine.

I remember when she couldn't talk. I remember the day I brought her home from the hospital to my house on Huaco Lane. I toted her around like a little doll, smirking with confidence that I could still fix a sandwich and hold an 7-pound baby at the same time. Looked like I had motherhood licked. It's in the can, folks. Call the game. I win.

OH MY GOD AND THEN I REALIZED *how in the world!?!?!....I can't do this!!!...someone please, hand me a nap and let me take a diaper!* Oh, those times I remember well.

Then this happened: College. Jobs. Marriage. Teacher. New house (in that order).

We have a bathtub now. We didn't have one at the old house, just a tiny stall shower that my great uncle installed on the fly with no instructions. But hey, it worked. We were grateful. Ava has a big room now with a place for all her toys. Our home is warm. It makes me cry. How strange.

I tried to keep my crying quiet, so as not to worry her. I just kept thinking of how she was when she was so small, trying to toddle across the floor. I remembered what it was like on her third birthday. And now, here she is, talking and having her own ideas and fears and wants. She's a tiny person. She's a little girl. I took a snapshot and filed it away in my "Death Bed Memory Box."

All of this is to say I don't know how to tell you what I want to tell you. Maybe I'm not supposed to share it. Fellow mothers will understand. The heart is a warm ocean and sometimes you hit an island with no name. It's there. It's very real and true; you just don't know what to call it. That's where I am. To keep me company, I have my favorite pirate. She's always been my First Mate. God surely is good for giving us a ship to make our way, oceans to explore, islands with no names, and each other to remind ourselves of how magical the voyage is.

III.

HOLD FAST
TO DREAMS

15. FEAR: A MONSTER FOR EVERYONE

Fear is a real bitch. Good thing it isn't you.

Rolling just underneath the surface of a hard, asphalt street, below the traffic noise bouncing off buildings and the meaningless chatter of everyday living, is a hushed monster. It is a sewer dweller. It is Fear.

Allow me to paint a picture. Fear is dressed in tattered black. Its face is twisted in a grimace and it sits along the wall, waiting for dreamed-up disasters. Occasionally, Fear speaks up and says, "Go here. Do this." Invariably, it is a bad idea. Can't really blame Fear though. It doesn't know any different. It just seeks relief from the panic inside Its chest. My chest is the asphalt street. The hidden places I don't talk about are the sewer. I try not to visit often in the hopes that I might forget about it.

Sometimes I'm not sure I have the weapons to kill that monster anyway.

I was cleaning out the closet that flooded from the AC. I was trying to move a huge, wire shelf full of clothes out of the narrowest door ever built by man when Fear showed up to call me a loser. Well, shit. Didn't It have something better to do? Like put a filter on like, a thousand Instagram posts?

I couldn't do it by myself. I kept shoving the shelf, which kept getting caught against the door frame. Life was not turning out how I planned. Of course, in Scarlett O'Hara fashion, I leaned against the wall and just started crying. *One day I'll have a house and I won't have AC problems!,* I thought. Oh my God. Dumb.

My Fear has a name that changes as often as the day. Sometimes I am afraid of being alone. Sometimes I am afraid of bugs. Sometimes I am afraid you will learn who I really am and I'll get kicked out of the club. Sometimes I am afraid of driving. Sometimes I am afraid of being hurt. Sometimes I am afraid I won't make it and I'll look like a fool and everyone will for sure laugh at me. And the friend my Fear has had the longest is the idea that I, just as I am, am unlovable and fundamentally broken. I don't talk about it because I'm afraid of you knowing.

I'm not the only one.

Fear tells me to go places and do things. If I get into a relationship, albeit dysfunctional and painful, at least I am not alone and someone loves me, thus seemingly eradicating that Fear that I am rejected by everyone. And then reality hits and I realize the solution Fear gave me caused more pain that I was willing to pay for. I cry. And Fear goes back to the corner, this time dragging me with it.

Fear asks, "what if?" And it's never "what if something amazing happens?" Fear is a bastard friend who I don't want at my party. I'm waiting for it to get bored and leave the house. But why would it when I provide so much interaction?

I am tired of this squeeze in my chest. I am tired of the loud, hollow reverb echoing off the glass of everyone else's life. I am tired of being a prisoner today.

Everything I know says: "Get out there and live." Everything says: "You aren't Fear. You aren't those things you heard." I wish there were more jokes for this. Being human means getting dirty and grappling with all my worldly ropes. I don't have to let them tie my wrists behind my back. I don't have to stay in the corner.

Maybe I'll go break a plate. Or maybe I'll utter one of those muffled prayers – the ones I sometimes feel like aren't heard. Maybe I'll tell someone I appreciate them. Maybe I'll meditate so much that my awareness cracks the ground above the sewer and sheds some white light on that tattered moron who lives below. Maybe I'll run hard and fast up the road through the trees until I find God.

This is life. It is mine. It isn't a rerun. It's live – in every way possible.

16. SELF-DOUBT: TOM FOOLERY'S EMOTIONALLY DAMAGED SECOND COUSIN

That feeling when you don't believe in yourself, but then you realize doubt is a shadow.

You don't believe in yourself. We get it.

That's what I'm waiting for everyone to say to me. Who's everyone? People, man. Just people.

I cut myself down first, then wait for others to follow suit. It's a skill I honed in high school. The idea is if I disassemble myself in front of everyone, no one else has to do it. And if they try, I've already affirmed them in their mission – so it's all good. Like water off a duck's back. You see that? You can't hurt me. I hurt myself first. We're all friends here.

But if you stuck a gun to my head and asked me, "Susan, do you think you're going to make it? Do you believe in yourself or not?" I'd scream "yassss!!!!!!!!!!" Then I'd ask why you're carrying a gun. Then I'd remember I'm in Texas.

I have a dream. A silly little dream of becoming a successful writer.

I use a veil of self-doubt to cover up what I believe others will see as foolish. I lack the courage to "dare greatly" sometimes, but I'm getting better at not giving a shit what other people think. The veil insulates me from ridicule:

Are you serious? You want to be a screenwriter?

Have you ever read your dialogue?

Hardly anyone ever really makes it. What's your Plan B?

But, you're not a good writer.

You suck, Susan. You suck at everything you do.

To think even for one second that you could make it in the world of writing – in any capacity at all – is not only a ludicrous proposition, but a dangerous one for both yourself and the reading population of this world. You and your silly, stupid, moronic dream should go step in front of a fast-moving train. Good day to you.

Now, no one has ever said these things to me. If they did, I'm sure I'd crawl into a small hole somewhere to sit in my hopelessness, I'd grow angry, then I'd pull myself back out with a Sasha Fierce/Beyoncé commitment to become successful *at them*. But the fear is that I'll exclaim my dream to anyone within earshot – which is what I want to do – then someone will read my writing and laugh at me.

This futile tango – swaying from being courageous about my aspirations to lightly mocking myself – has gotten better over the years. Like I said, my give-a-damn dwindles with each day I grow older. Maybe that's desperation setting in, but it seems letting go of the need for approval is a much smoother way to live and operate in the world.

And I think this is relevant because everyone lives with the small voice that says in some form or fashion: "You can't."

And that, friends, is a story created in our heads. The authors of my "Can't Story" are those bastards in high school, odds, the need for approval, fear, and me. It's an exhausting, unforgiving piece of fiction that pops up every now and then.

Hey dickheads, I can.

Way back when, in some scuzzy flat in Edinburgh, J.K. Rowling was a single mom on welfare when she completed the first book in the Harry Potter series. It was rejected by 8 publishers.

At one point, Walt Disney was so broke that he had to eat dog food. His first successful cartoon character was ripped off by Universal, and MGM told him nobody would like Mickey Mouse.

Van Gogh sold one painting in his lifetime, but completed over 800. And he whacked his ear off, but I think that was because he was probably on his period.

Winston Churchill lost in every election until he was elected Prime Minister, then helped lead Great Britain through the bloodiest war the world had ever seen.

Before Sidney Poitier won an Oscar and 3 Golden Globes (nearly ten nominations for both awards – not including the wins), a casting director at his first audition suggested, "Why don't you stop wasting people's time and go out and become a dishwasher or something?"

The only reason I'm mentioning these people now is because they didn't let a little (or a lot of) doubt eat them and their dream alive. The world can be a cold, scary, cruel place – not conducive to nurturing warm fantasies of how you might live and contribute happiness to the world. And many go out into this storm, meet the wild wind of uncertainty, and let it blow them far away from the place their heart intended.

Fear and doubt are little gremlins that have as much authority as I allow them. It's depressing to think about how full the graveyard is with people who gave up, how different the world might be if we didn't set up our own impenetrable ceilings.

"Everybody needs something to hang their hat on." That's what my friend said during a conversation we were having about careers in filmmaking. He chose to hang his hat on directing. He owns his ability, his passion, his goal, his dream. His conviction is so cemented that if you told him pursuing a career in filmmaking is waste of time, he'd flip you the bird and laugh all the way to his next shoot. The dude is as bold as they come.

I need something to hang my hat on. I need an unwavering, zealous belief in my dream. I also need to say – and this is just for me – that I don't want to care about what anyone thinks. I've chosen writing. And since I'm dramatic, I'm laying claim to this here. Cue the lights, hit the music, and hear me when I say:

I want to be a writer. I'm going to make it.

One of my favorite things to do is talk to people about what their dream is. If I'm talking to a kid, I try to forewarn them of the dangers of conformity. "Don't do what your parents want you to do. You want to start a garage band? Do it." And I always leave these conversations feeling glad. There's relief in encouraging people to join me in the chase for something that at times seems out of reach.

I wish I had more Zig Ziglar-inspired things to say about how to be successful and overcome these bumps that threaten to take dreams out. Spoiler alert: I don't. I just have my own personal experience with wanting something so bad, and wrestling with my Can't Monster. It's Tom Foolery to think I can't or won't make it.

Weave it into existence – thread after thread, day after day, no matter how many times you prick your finger on the needle. The story is that you can't. The reality is that you can.

Oh, the places I'll go!...if I get out of my own way. From one zealous human being to another, here's to hoping your dream never dies. The Can't Monster that feeds on fear and doubt is committed to seeing it dead, and it's your job to keep it alive. Fight for it.

Oh, one last thing. If your dream is to be an axe murderer, ignore everything you just read.

IV.

CLEOPATRA

17. SOLDIER ON, HUMAN

This was how I told everyone I was getting divorced again. You know, after I overcame the negative self-talk and the overwhelming feeling of shame. Peace was found in the thought of others.

I'm getting divorced. Again.

Whew, there I said it. It doesn't roll off my tongue like I thought it would. It rings out more like a drunken cymbal player in a marching band full of people tripping acid. Great. It's my life.

I was so embarrassed for a while. I hoped no one would ask about it for at least another ten years, that way when people heard what happened, they wouldn't have to know that the divorce was filed just days before our one-year anniversary. I feel like that's an appropriate time for a divorce. Ten years. Maybe 15. Any time after that you might as well stay together because you'll both be dead soon anyway.

I told myself the following: *Susan, you're a writer – a wild, creative bird – and birds like you have wacky lives like this. They get divorced twice before they're 30.* It's how I reconciled myself with disappointment and pain.

So anyway, there I was in the middle of a warm furnace of self-pity balled up in the fetal position. I rolled around, consumed with thoughts about myself, my pain, my anger, my bitterness, my life, my future…my, my, my.

This mortgage! How will I pay it? I am but a lowly public-school teacher!

dramatic sigh

It was my turn goddammit. I've already paid my Single Mom dues!

dramatic wail

Who will buy me a Christmas present now?! I work so hard and I deserve a salon gift certificate!

dramatic nose blowing

It was in this ridiculous mess of miserable, pathetic happenings that I realized: OH MY GOD. I AM NOT THE ONLY PERSON ON THIS PLANET.

A long time ago, I had the divine inspiration to write Christmas cards to strangers as a way of throwing a little good in the world where there is otherwise a lot of pain and nastiness. I don't tell you that to shed light on what a wonderful person I am, though I know that's exactly what you're thinking. I write that to set up what my morning was like today.

We had an "unresolvable visitation issue" this Thanksgiving, so Ava was not here this morning. She won't be at lunch with my family and I haven't told them yet. I couldn't sleep last night. When I woke up at a decent enough hour to start thinking, sweet, delicious waves of self-pity began to roll out of my eyes. Oh! The humanity! Red alert. Red alert. Danger zone. Whatever.

I sulked my way to the kitchen, made coffee, and then broke out the box of Christmas cards I bought on sale last year. I opened them, dusting myself and the couch with the glitter from the cover. Each card read "Happy Holidays" and I thought about how people fight about that. Then I thought, *people are stupid.*

75

I began writing to a stranger. The cards started out serious:

"The world can be a scary, dark place…. ISIS….war…. but don't forget that it's also beautiful."

As the writing went on, I began to get a little silly. I told people my circumstance, and as per my usual, I cracked a few jokes about it. I wrote about God loving all of us, even if we don't think so. I wrote about how we're all here doing stupid, beautiful things and we just have to be nice to one another. And I signed each with: "Regards, another human being."

I started thinking about Syrian refugee camps. Who am I to cry this morning? I felt so much anger and hurt with my head on the pillow, but now…. now I was aware again that I'm not the center of the universe. I was aware that there are people who are truly suffering and I had a choice. I could either throw anger and bitterness on top of my heart today and walk out the door of my house into the war outside with that banner waving, or I could try to do something, however small, to make the world a little less disgusting.

I don't like that in many places on this planet there are people fleeing danger to save the lives of their families. If I can't take them into my own home, which I absolutely would, I can at least not be a bitch to the people in my own town. I can celebrate what I have. I can throw anger down a forgotten well, at least for today, and see where I can help. Just for today.

I have so much. People like me don't have houses or custody of our kids. We don't sit in an uncomfortable feeling and try to find peace. We don't love and we don't think of others. But God rearranged all that. God picked me up where I was and put me on New Land. Today, I have a home. I have a job that lets me be of service to others. My daughter has never seen me drink. I am alive, and somewhere in my heart, I have that human commodity that could change the whole world and that we don't use enough: Love.

So, things didn't work out. So, it went a little sideways. I'm used to it. I'm still walking. No need to worry.

Today, I can make the world better. Today, I can be grateful. And Lord knows, there will be enough pie to put me to sleep if I feel like I can't make it.

18. CONSIDER THE DAMN LILY – PART I

Divorce is never fun, but that's not what the clerks at the courthouse think.

Cheap, dull lighting hung overhead from a dusty chandelier in an old house-turned-lawyer's-office on a busy street in town. Papers were piled in every free space – people's lives, their mistakes, their futures, and their regrets were written in tiny fine print on lily-white pages. All over. It was a mess. A half-broken chair leaned against the wall in the corner, complete with a duct taped arm rest.

An overweight old guy – someone who looked like Santa, if Santa had caught a DWI in his mid-forties and never recovered from his legal separation from Mrs. Claus – this dude right here was my official assistant. He had the knowledge and Word document templates full of legal jargon that I needed to undo my own mistake. I hated this guy from the minute I saw him.

My divorce hearing was set for January 15, 2016, a Friday. The broken, depressed Santa had made the arrangements I needed. Papers had been filed. Tomorrow, I would sit in front of a judge to say, "Whoops."

I made a few loose, mental resolutions this year.

Maybe I'll give up sugar.

Maybe I'll save more money.

Maybe I'll pray that one kickass prayer I know every day and see how it changes my life.

I landed with the sugar thing because this divorce has left me on the fluffy side, and sometimes you just have to lose weight AT people, you know? That lasted about sixteen hours on New Year's Day and then I accidentally ran into some red velvet cake. I ate three pieces, but they were small so it's okay.

Dammit! I'm not going to do this shit again this year, I thought to myself. I'm not going to shoot out my own knee caps because I eat cake. I'm not going to yell at my naked reflection. I'm not going to get mad when I look at pictures of Charlize Theron and Scarlett Johansson.

I'm not going to stick a toothbrush down my throat. I'm not going to hurt myself on purpose. I'm not going to let my internal voice go on destructive rants, big or small:

You're not good enough. You're ugly. You're old and gross. You're unwanted. You're broken. You're wrong.

Not this year.

And then I came up with a resolution.

The relationship I was making my way out of left me carved out. I was so entranced, infused, surrounded and controlled by fear and shame that I wasn't familiar with myself anymore. I sold off pieces of myself over the years, little plots of land here and there, for real cheap. I found myself at the opening of 2016 in a stressed shell of skin, hopeful and broken in turns.

My simple resolution floated to the surface without any fanfare or glitter.

This year, I'm going to love myself.

I'm going to love myself if I go running. I'm going to love myself if I wear workout clothes and eat pizza. I'm going to love myself if I succeed. I'm going to love myself if I fail. I'm going to reject my poisonous self-criticism and change my internal narrative. That is what I resolve to do this year.

The morning of the hearing went as smooth as you'd expect. I wore all black and listened to *Call to Arms* by Dropkick Murphys on the way to the courthouse. I was running a little behind.

The court coordinator was extremely chipper and kind when I arrived to the 170th District court room. Her aura was warm velvet all around me. I wondered how she could work that job and maintain that kind of attitude. The judge was equally pleasant. I swore in, and I made it a point to say "YES" instead of "I do" when he asked me if the testimony I was about to give was true and correct, so help me God. I smiled as much as possible and made polite conversation when he realized he knew my family. Inside I felt a tinge of embarrassment for my sweet dad. My mistake suddenly felt very official.

When it was over, he agreed to grant my divorce. He does this all day. I wrapped up the loose ends with the district clerk and emerged from the court house into the unusually warm January air. The sun was spreading its light over the buzzing downtown of my city. And just like that, I was Susan Duty again.

I let the sun whisper its hope. I let myself feel what I felt. I let myself be me, in all my glorious (and official) whoopsy daisies. I let myself be human and I didn't whip my spirit for my decisions. I breathed in and I exhaled.

The journey that I've decided to embark on this year hasn't begun with wrapping arms around myself or singing affirmations as I put on eyeliner in the morning. So far, it has involved letting myself be entirely who I am at the moment. It has involved drinking juice. It has involved a lot of simple prayers and nicotine patches.

I feel like I'm at a base camp looking up at the snow caps of a mountain many miles above my head. I don't know when I constructed this place. Maybe it was when I lied about my weight in fourth grade. I'm sure I added some structures when I started doing drugs to escape the reality I couldn't stand. I know the negative, toxic, sad environment I found myself in at the end of my marriage wasn't entirely a product of that union. It had begun long ago. But this year, I'm going to love myself no matter what.

It is my intention to leave this place and ascend the mountain to figure out who I'm supposed to be. I want to leave the camp that doesn't work, and everything else, where it belongs: behind me.

Burn the basecamp. Let's go.

19. CONSIDER THE DAMN LILY –

PART II

When you worry about money because you don't have any and apparently, it's a part of life.

"What I'm trying to do here is to get you to relax, to not be so preoccupied with getting, so you can respond to God's giving. People who don't know God and the way he works fuss over these things, but you know both God and how he works. Steep your life in God-reality, God-initiative, God-provisions. Don't worry about missing out. You'll find all your everyday human concerns will be met."

Matthew 6:31-33, The Message

Gritty dust covers the tops of black frames sitting in a home depot box in the living room. The built-in bookcase, such a cute and delighted-in detail of the house I was excited about a year and a half ago, is now long planks of primer-white bare bone. Pictures are gone. Knick knacks are put away. The books have been sorted into a "keep" pile and a "yard sale" pile. It's the end, and my props are going back in their suitcases to prepare for another adventure.

I can't afford to live here anymore.

There is a part of me that hates the reality of all this. It sounds cliché to say it wasn't part of my plan. The pain of uttering that phrase is no match for the lingering, stinging regret that still salts up my spirit. I wish I had made different choices, but I didn't.

There's a payment on Ava's student lunch account due. One of my student loans is on deferment. The car is acting up. The fridge is making a clicking noise that sounds like a couple hundred-dollar repair. There's too much and I feel like I'm drowning. Maybe Bernie Sanders is right. The middle class is dying. Am I middle class? Maybe I'm just me.

I want to throw fire at capitalism and our shitty economy. I want to blame big banks and student loan people for my enslavement. I want everything to be everyone's fault. I want to crawl into a small hole underneath the house, set up a makeshift camp, and tell the department of education when they come looking for me that I'm defecting to communist Russia and I'll send them a post card when I land.

But consider the damn lilies.

"And why do you worry about clothes? See how the flowers of the field grow. They do not labor or spin. Yet I tell you that not even Solomon in all his splendor was dressed like one of these. If that is how god clothes the grass of the field, which is here today and tomorrow is thrown into the fire, will he not much more clothe you— you of little faith?"

Matthew 6:28-30

Oh, me of little faith. I'm long past worrying about clothes. I worry about the fridge though. God takes care of the world and it's easy for me to see that, but then I forget that includes the house on my street that I call my home. Somehow, I separate myself from the world in times like this. I feel adrift on an island – a shitty, manmade island of broken bottles and empty cat food bags. Here I am, floating somewhere down the river of life, watching all of you safely on shore. Happy for you. Glad to hear it. My cat food bag island is an illusion. I'm one of god's kids, too.

I've been putting myself back together. My marriage was abusive in every sense of the word. I just recently came to terms with that and felt bold enough to tell someone. So many secrets, so many props, so many stage directions. I forgot who I was. I lost myself. I became a temple for fear and frustration, sorrow and remorse. I was a captive, a P.O.W., until one day I fell over the falls and committed to getting out of it despite the fear that spit and snarled and swiped its claws at my ankles.

I started boxing. I set goals for myself and made it a point to reach them. This was for two reasons: 1) to feel like I was worth a shit, 2) to see how far the power of God could take me. I knew if I were to do anything difficult, it was going to be because God helped me do it. I was such a shell when this journey began. All my energy was gone. It took everything to get started.

Last Saturday morning, I woke up and put my running shoes on. I prayed for God to help me in the race I was about to run. I got out of the truck on a dirt road in the middle of an open field, wearing all black, ready for what was coming. It was Tough Mudder day. I showed up smiling, ran in the mud (and later in the rain). I was pulled from mud pits and then turned to help someone else out of the same mess. I finished at a full run, bright eyed and dirty. Life. It has been well over half a year since I fell over the falls.

"So do not worry, saying, 'what shall we eat?' or 'what shall we drink?' or 'what shall we wear?' for the pagans run after all these things, and your Heavenly Father knows that you need them. But

seek first his kingdom and his righteousness, and all these things will be given to you as well."

    Matthew 6:25-34

20. SNUGGIES AND OTHER ATTEMPTS AT LIFE

It's okay to be a little messed up after you get divorced. You don't have to spring back like a jeans model after their first kid.

Who's going to turn down hot cheese pizza and a Harry Potter marathon? Nobody. At least nobody I want to be friends with. Yeah, 2016 is a new year. I'm turning over a new leaf. Just as soon as I'm done shoving this congealed flour and dairy in my mouth. What's that sound? Oh, and I'm crying? Whatever, bros. Since when do I give a damn?

Dammit. I always give a damn. I've got the gene for feeling the feelings.

Let's add that I've been in adult footie jammies pretty much every day this entire winter break. I'm 30.

If I could just get the lioness without to match the lioness within, I might look like someone who hasn't given up right now. It's ok though. I bought a juicer.

I feel like people want to pump you full of tiger pictures with fanciful quote overlays around this time of year. Talkin' about scars. Talkin' about the fight. Why can't we just lay around in a Snuggie and feel just as much like a warrior?

I feel like that's part of the process, isn't it? When things take a turn for Shitville and you find yourself caught between a mother fucker and a wacky spot, aren't you supposed to just sit there and be beautifully imperfect for a minute? You know, before you get a gym membership you won't actually use?

Here's something I said yesterday: "Whatever. I'm gonna lose like a thousand pounds and get famous." And I said this with a mouthful of dough, all while eyeing a pecan pie that my mother foolishly thought she'd send home with me to save for Christmas. Ha. That pie won't make it.

No one wants to talk about how hilariously disgusting it can be when you're nursing yourself back to health. But it's real and true, brothers and sisters. And it's ok.

I'm not here to be your Tony Robbins. I'm here to tell you that if you want to eat pizza in footie jammies and try your juicer out tomorrow, you can. I just want to tell you it's ok to be a warthog while you wait for your lioness to get back on her feet. Whatever it is you need to do to get back to your fighting weight, it's ok. As long as it's not murder. Don't do that.

21. CRYING IN PUBLIC

A memory from a long time ago creeped up when I was on the stair machine. And then I melted into a beautiful mess at Planet Fitness.

I have to write this because that's the best way for me to clear swirly, emotional thunderstorms off the horizon of my day. And I intend on having the best day humanly possible, because this is the only July 8, 2017 I'll ever get.

I was at the gym minding my own business, half set on getting a fitness model body and half set on just being healthy, when suddenly, the WIC office popped in my head. For those who don't know, the WIC office is where you go when you're pregnant or have a tiny baby that you need help feeding, because your income is not enough.

For the longest time, I didn't realize that people thought I was rich because my dad owns a pizza place that's been open for 48 years. When I got sober, I became pretty set on not taking anything from my parents anymore. So Rollo's money was not my money, unless you count the paycheck I received from working 40 hours a week at a shade above minimum-wage. I wanted to be responsible for myself and I wanted to live the right way, which in my mind meant not asking my mom and dad for anything.

So there I was, 23-years-old, pregnant with a little girl, and all alone. I worked my 40 hours a week and all my money went to paying the electric bill, the water bill, blah blah blah, etc. etc. So there was a time in my life when I couldn't quite make it all work by myself and I needed a little assistance. This meant going down to that office and sitting for hours until I was called back, which I hated for many reasons. One was just time and inconvenience and the other was pride.

As I played around with a machine I wasn't quite sure how to work, the memory of that office popped in my head for no real reason at all. I felt the familiar, salty wetness of remembrance well up in the corner of my eye. *That was a hard time*, I thought.

This thought was the engine of a train I didn't expect to be on today. And before I knew it I was thinking of those times in college, when Ava was learning her letters and I was learning about Reconstruction. My school schedule was organized around daycare availability. Yes, there were late nights reading and trying to soothe a baby who was teething. Yes, there were times when she got sick and I had to just figure it out. There was a dysfunctional relationship in that time, too, which has its own dusty box of dark memories.

And then I remembered Baylor. By this point in the Yesterday Train adventure at Planet Fitness, I am full on crying. I mean tears rolling down my face IN A PUBLIC PLACE, and I still don't really know why. I just had this very warm wash over my whole body that, if it could speak, would say, *"That was a lot of hard stuff, Susan. I can't believe you did it."*

I briefly thought about my old house in the suburbs that I bought with my ex-husband. I remember thinking during that time I had really made it in life. And then I remember the day I left it. I was standing in the front door looking back at the entryway that I had painted a pretty red color. As I cried over what I presumed a failure on my part, I just said, "Goodbye, house. Thanks." And then I turned the lock for the last time.

That loss, that relationship all together, that inevitable divorce, that feeling was also hard. And then the warm wash said again, "Good God, you made it!"

I figured I should leave the gym, because I was done working out and because I wasn't sure how to answer the question I figured I'd be asked: "Ma'am, are you ok? Also, you think you're done with this stair machine, because I also need to work my glutes so I can feel confident today."

I took that whole damn experience, in all its unexpectedness, and I said to myself, "I am going to make it. I am going to get through anything life gives me because that's my experience so far. And one day I will be a paid writer and I will buy a house for Ava and me. And I won't be in a relationship that hurts. And I will be as strong as a woman can possibly be."

I got in my car and I drove away to write this. I know I'm not the only one with this story. Maybe some of the characters are different. Maybe your setting isn't the same. But other women have a theme that's tied to mine. Belief in the impossible keeps me alive. And dammit, I can affirm that it has already happened for me. I know, I really know, it can still happen. I am strong and I don't give up. I may throw a fit and I may cuss a lot, but I keep going.

Feels good to be alive and where I am. I think I'll keep my little memories and take my unnecessary baggage off the train right here and throw it in the Brazos. I won't need it where I'm going anyway. You won't either.

V.

HOLD EVEN FASTER TO DREAMS BECAUSE WE'RE GOING BROKE

22. UP SHARK CREEK WITHOUT A COMPASS

What to do when you don't know what to do and other things about sharks.

I am no more certain about where my life is going than cattle are about where they're headed when they leave the farm. Achievement unlocked. One point for the easy-goers.

I used to have such purpose, such a drive to succeed. When the mouth of the river appeared and I was swept rather unceremoniously into the ocean, I met my new position with an extended fit of crying. Science calls it depression. Whatever. They were right.

I found a solution to that problem, and I'm damn grateful for that.

Here I float in the ocean of adulthood, somewhere between 18 and 40, happy for the raft I have and clueless as to where the hell that map went. It's here somewhere, or isn't. Maybe a shark ate it. Oh, I've known a shark or two.

The sun on the horizon is the same it's always been. Ever faithful, it rises and falls without a recognition of my complaints or questions. Oh, this silly ocean, these currents, and this damned floating.

When you feel like you've lost your compass, it's easy to start spending your time mulling over the problems you have. If you're a sailor and you've lost your compass, you're double screwed. My raft isn't in the best condition, and my telescope went the way of the map – probably in

the belly of a tiger shark because those
anything.

It was in this season of alternating between panic,
depression, and malaise that I gave up. I surrendered to
the weight of the atmosphere, snuggled up in my raft, and
by accident, found a sense of peace unlike any I had ever
known.

It was *because* I had lost my compass that I became
open to the islands on the horizon. Suddenly, I was
wrapped up in a tingling air of grace. Potential popped all
around me, and I was no longer responsible for solving all
the problems of my life in one day. In fact, I realized I had
no problems at all. Everything was as it should be.

"Not all those who wander are lost" is a hippie-
bumper-sticker quote that I've always appreciated. But the
peace came in recognizing I wasn't lost. I had to admit that
to myself. And this whole time I thought that quote was to
absolve stoners from having to tell their parents when
they're going to get a real job! My ship is merely on a
different heading and moving at a different clip. Well,
that's a much different set of circumstances than my
previous perspective suggested.

It's all good. I still write. I'm getting a day job. I still
dream. I still think of screenplays and television scripts. I
love my raft. And should I ever come across that shark
that I presume ate all my necessary equipment, I'll try to
remember to thank him.

23. AN INVITATION TO PASSION AND A SHOUTOUT TO ZEALOTS

Pull. The. Trigger.

Sit down, we need to talk. It was after a long, arduous summer day of doing odd jobs for my dad that my mom decided to reward us with a trip to the movies. This was the usual reward when we were out of school. It was 1995, and Ron Howard's *Apollo 13* was dominating theaters across the country. I walked into that movie theater a fairly normal 10-year-old. The film began to roll and I sat still, excited for the story about to unfold.

I remember the exact moment it happened. It was the scene where the rocket broke away from the icy machinery holding it on the launch pad and Jim Lovell, played by the incomparable Tom Hanks, told his crew the "clock is running." The film's score began to swell as the rocket shook violently and then began its powerful ascension into the heavens.

It was right there, right then, that I realized a projector was behind me and that strangers were in the theater with me. I knew this was a movie, and the feeling I had for the crew onscreen – the undeniable emotion I was sharing with people I didn't know – was orchestrated by "movie people." In that theater seat in 1995, my dream was born.

I left with the resolution that one day when I grew up, that's what I would do with my life. I was going to be in the movies. *Apollo 13* is still my favorite movie for this very reason.

Later I learned what a screenwriter was. It seemed like the perfect fit for me. I took my allowance and bought screenwriting books. I read them in my AP English class instead of paying attention. I skipped school to write at Cameron Park a lot.

Now, active alcoholism took up many years of my life. I tried to continue my love for writing while in the throes of that disease, but one can only drink so much liquor before you're too drunk to press the keys on a keyboard in the right order.

I got sober, and a few years later after I had Ava, I realized my goal of going to film school was going to slip away if I didn't go after it. There was a sense of urgency as I watched my 6-month-old daughter sit in a cracker box while I managed my dad's pizza joint.

My dream of being a screenwriter was always there. It has never, ever left my spirit. For a few years it was just a lump in my throat. It was the neighbor you were letting stay in the basement. You knew he was there, but you didn't pay much attention. But that neighbor played a steady drum – a low, pulsing, life-giving thud. The telltale heart!

I graduated with a film degree, of which I am most proud, in December of 2013. Before I left Baylor, I won a screenwriting contest and $300 which I used to take my daughter on our first real vacation.

Life kicked in after that and I got married and bought a house. When he decided suburban life really wasn't for him, I divorced. I had begun a career as an English teacher and was grateful for the money I had. I stayed in the house for as long as I could, desperate to give my daughter the life I thought she deserved, until the day finally came when I realized I could not afford it on my own. I sold the house and started a new chapter of my life in the one-bedroom apartment behind my mom and dad's house. It was humbling. Still is.

And then, after a few months of spirit stirring, I came into a clearing. There was a cliff in front of me. To my back were the monsters of life, hungry for dreams and all that is beautiful about being an idealist. Trump got elected, my job's requirements seemed impossible to satisfy, and there wasn't a house open for me to buy in my price range. I felt like I was on a plank, and on this plank with my legs quivering under an unforgiving reality, I heard something say "jump."

Today, on February 1st, I gave my boss a letter of intent. I told her I would not be returning for the 2017-2018 school year. I have decided to use the money I have saved to fund myself for one year while I do nothing but write. It sounds crazy because it is.

When I am 80-years-old and thumbing through the pages of my life, I will not be the woman in the wheelchair who says, "I wish I would have." I can accept trying and failing, but I will not accept that I didn't give all of myself for the dream that came to life in 1995. I will return to the Earth knowing I went at this full force, with all my wild atoms in synch. That will be my story.

Most people have been supportive. I left work today almost shaking. I also had a hazy vision of holding the hand of God. I believe He gave me this thing. It would be easier I think if my dream was to become an accountant, but that is not the case with me.

I have a specific project I am working on. It came to me a few years ago and I recently picked it back up.

I write all of this to tell you I'm scared, to tell you that your love and your passion will also lead you to do crazy things. It will take you to crossroads and bridges. It will thump under your floor boards until you cry out or mercilessly kill it with doubt. But I don't want mine to die. Langston Hughes wrote, "Hold fast to dreams, for if dreams die life is broken-winged bird that cannot fly." I want to use the wings God gave me. And they better work, because I just pulled the trigger and sprinted off that cliff I mentioned. The wind will surely catch me. It always has.

24. A LONG ROAD WITH THE KIND BAPTISTS

You'll go a long way, baby.

Lots of people don't participate in the graduation ceremony that's held at the end of four years of college. My mom was one of those people. This has always baffled me. Why wouldn't you celebrate such an arduous journey with a ten second stroll in the spotlight? Hell, I'll take a spotlight any way I can get it. I'm just relieved this one isn't attached to a police cruiser.

I didn't go to college right out of high school, but I sure told everyone I was going. That was the natural order of things after all. I didn't have the heart to tell all the people who weren't the least bit concerned with my plans that I was too high to fill out the application. And if I wasn't high, I was too petrified to do what everyone else was doing. I have always been semi-obsessed with living a very picturesque Americana existence, and I really did want to go to college. In my mind, I decided the University of North Texas was the place for me. I never printed out an application or took the SATs. College was just a cloudy place in the back of my head, a fantasy, a daydream. Something to keep me feeling like I fit in.

I just barely graduated high school and entered the exciting world of waiting tables. At my new job I met a gem of a human being who dealt meth in the wee hours of the night when he wasn't busy smoking weed. It was okay though because he just sold to his friends. He had a lot of friends. Shack Crack turned out to be a passing phase for me. I'm a downer kind of girl.

After rocking and rolling for about a year in the drug scene I had grown very comfortable in, I met a nice guy who I married after knowing him for four months. How romantic. Drinking at this time was what it'd always been — a lot of fun most of the time and sometimes kind of dangerous. No big deal. I was young. I was in love. I was optimistic.

I can't tell you how or why it happened, but at some point during the course of that marriage the thrash of alcoholism got a little wilder than what I was used to handling. Slowly and painfully, I started losing pieces of myself in the whipping and wailing that began to accompany my drinking more and more. And I was drinking every day. I always wrote during this time — except when the keys mysteriously got smaller and started swaying side to side. Then I just watched M*A*S*H and dreamed up some pretty amazing acceptance speeches.

By this point in my imagined career, drinking had become very necessary. I took a few trips to try and shake myself out of it. I dabbled in Buddhism for a while — which really meant I just smoked weed all the time and told everyone I was Buddhist. When I'd wake up, I would tell myself that I wouldn't drink. Sounded simple enough. Sometimes I'd make it all the way to ten in the morning. I was in a real pickle. Dark, damp and dismal was the dungeon I wallowed in, mournful for a time when things didn't seem so bad. I shot up a flare. Send help.

The rest of the story is reserved for a group of my select friends. Point is, I eventually stopped drinking. On March 7, 2008, I woke up in a sterile detox joint that smelled like the nurse's office in elementary school. Since that mild spring morning, I haven't put alcohol or any other narcotics in my body. To this very day, no one has thrown me a parade. Ungrateful bastards. All of you.

Feeling much better physically and having a newfound clarity, I thought it'd be a good idea to go to college. Maybe it wasn't too late to live the dream. That was August of 2008. I took nine hours at the local community college and felt like a real smart girl because I did really well. Oh, and I got divorced. I'm still friends with my ex-husband. We just decided there were too many issues to deal with. We were also still in our early twenties so we didn't know what the hell we were doing.

The following spring, I didn't return to school. I was just going to work at my parents' restaurant and write a screenplay. But what actually happened was I got pregnant. Some guy I dated for thirty seconds. Didn't want to continue dating . Big plus sign on the stick. Alone. The end.

See how I avoided my martyrdom there? Maybe I deserve a cake? Maybe?

And for the next fifteen months I managed a pizza joint, grew a human being in my body, delivered that human being, and then I practiced being responsible for the next six months. Ava was sitting in a shiny new buss tub that my dad and I had converted into a mobile-crib-thing when it hit me: *If I don't go after my dream right now, I never will. And Jesus Christ, why is my kid in a buss tub?*

I enrolled again at the community college. After three happy semesters there, I transferred to Baylor University in August of 2011.

As proud as I was to be going to *THE* Baylor University, I hated it. All the labels I attached to myself really clashed with the preconceived notions I held about this private institution of higher education (and Baptists in general). I just kept thinking, *I'm not joining a life group.* I also clearly remember wanting to mock everything and everyone by crowding up the "chalk talk" around campus with a thrilling announcement about the "new, very exciting Unwed Mothers Club" which would meet at the Spiritual Life Center on a very exciting night — provided everyone could find babysitters. Happily for the administration and the Asians for Christ group, I got over myself pretty quickly. (Seriously, AFC has notes everywhere on the sidewalk. There's not enough space to compete. It's weird.)

All totaled, I've spent five whole semesters at Baylor with a summer stint at MCC in between to make up for lost time. Along the way I read lots of textbooks to Ava, which has given her a rather expanded vocabulary for a four-year-old. I've been puked on before important final exams. Late nights of studying and writing led to early mornings of worrying that I didn't do enough. Somewhere in between, Ava grew up a lot.

The thing I've consistently bitched about has been missing a lot of her childhood because of "educational activities." The only thing I had to soothe myself was the thought that someday this would all be worth it. Someday, I'd be able to get off "guvunment aid" and provide for both of us. Someday, I'd be a writer and we'd have a nice life of health insurance and grocery money.

Now, you better believe I'm a writer already. Uh,

hello? I'm doing it right now. But payment is another story. I did win some money at Baylor's Black Glasses Film Festival for a screenplay I wrote. I used it to take Ava on the vacation I promised her. The overnight visit to Galveston that we took this past summer was one of the happiest times of my life. I felt like a really good mom. With the car loaded up with a cooler, towels and beach toys, we made the five-hour trip to the coast in June. The smell of ocean water was as I remembered it when my mom and dad took me decades before. In fact, Galveston smelled the same way it did that night I gave up. Now a sober mother, taking my kid on the vacation I told her we'd take, I felt like a solid success in some small way, rather than the half-running, directionless dreamer I had been before. I took her out to eat and bought her a shirt. We built some sandcastles and let the warm waves tickle our bellies as we sat on the pressed, finely crushed pieces of earth that made up the beach. Just thinking about it now makes me tear up a little. Without Baylor, I wouldn't have had that experience.

Graduation is in 45 days.

All of this is to say that you bet your persistently reading ass I'm going to that ceremony. Whoever is charged with the responsibility of watching Ava that day will bring her down to the bottom railing of the Ferrell Center when my name is about to be called. And in between those green, metal bars she'll see me in a cap and gown, walking across some plywood stage to shake the hand of the man that wanted to kick Bill Clinton out of the White House for doing what presidents do best. I don't know if she'll remember it, but I think her spirit will. It's without a doubt the longest walk I've ever taken, next to getting sober.

It's important for her to see this. I want her to know that women are more than silhouettes and eyelashes. I want her to see that dreaming big is hard, but big dreams are possible. I want her to always remember her mind is the most powerful weapon in a world that wants to tell her plastic body parts will take you far. I want her to know deep down in her gut that falling off doesn't mean falling out. Hope is always just a few steps away. Send up a flare if you need to.

She's been so patient with me. Everyone has. As I near this very important date, unsure of my future, I can only whisper prayers of sincere gratitude for the Divine Energy that helped me along the way. I didn't die on the living room floor that one Christmas several years ago. I didn't miscarry my pregnancy. All the events of my life that I thought were so backwards and misplaced were how they were supposed to be. So it has been for eons before my arrival on this planet, and so it will be long after I go down to dust and dreams.

I can sit back and remember it all. I'm alive. I think of the hardships, the work, the joy, the triumph, the soulful ring of a job well done. I've taken it all in stride. I need not worry. Mountains may crumble and rain might fall, but it doesn't matter anymore. I can sit back and think, *Whew, we really have come a long way, baby.* Flares and all.

VI.
WELL, SINCE WE'RE AMONG THE LIVING

25. THE ART OF THE CARDIGAN

I want to age gracefully, like Meryl Streep, but in all likelihood I will do it with much less dignity and certainly less Oscar nominations.

Look, here's the deal, all of my feelings can basically be classified in two major mood groups: "Punch Things" and "Hug Things." Some people want to get technical and call this Bi-Polar, but whatever. I ain't diagnosed, playa. And anyway, I think it's applicable to all humanity. We have love and hate. We have good and evil. Are you trying to tell me the fundamental nature of all mankind is bi-polar? It would help explain Sean Spicer, but that doesn't make it a fact. (For reimbursement of cheap jokes, please see the man behind the curtain.)

Here lately, I've been putting a lot of things in the "Punch Things" column. Maybe it's the moon, maybe it's Maybelline. I haven't quite figured it out, but I know this one thing: I'm not 22 anymore.

I caught my reflection in the window of my car today and scared myself. I'm just this side of a minivan and mom shorts. At first I thought it was the thick, baggy, black cardigan that was making me look old. It screams middle age at the pitch of a pissed off four-year-old. But I like it because it's warm, not very clingy, and it was free. My sister-in-law gave it to me along with a whole bag full of want-me-nots. But in the right light, the cardigan makes me look professional. And professional isn't old. So it's not the cardigan.

Maybe it's my hair. I have a forehead you can land a plane on and uncovered it makes me look a little bit like

Rocky Dennis. I have bangs for two reasons: my love of the retro look and, more importantly, to avoid looking like Rocky Dennis. I guess sometimes I look older because of my style. I used sponge rollers the other night for God's sake. But I know it's not the hair.

If it's not the hair or my clothes, it has to be my skin. My friend's high-resolution camera pointed out my crow's feet the other day. I hadn't noticed them before, but there they are, plain as day. It must mean I've done a lot of smiling. Little lines jut out from the corners of my eyes like they have a point to make, like they have something to say! Obviously, this means I've lived a life of deep laughter. And I smoke. Oh God, is it my skin?

It's weird to notice yourself aging.

Why am I talking about this? Virgin ears, be warned. It's here that you'll want to depart. I can't be held responsible for your feelings about the next several paragraphs.

Media can take their impossible beauty ideals for women and shove them straight up their Pilates toned, perfectly defined [expletive redacted by editor]. "Up against the wall, mother fucker." You're the problem. (Expletive retained for emphasis.)

The average Victoria's Secret model is 5'10 and 110 pounds. I'm 5'7 and 145 pounds on a good day. I was chubby growing up and kids at school were always good at reminding me. I lost 50 pounds in between my junior and senior year of high school. Even now, I have curves and lots of meat on my bones. And I should say that I'm absolutely fine with the way I look. I'd go so far as to say I love my body. This is good, because it's the only one I got.

My problem is this: I live in a world clamoring for me to do, have, and *be* more. The message is so pervasive in our culture that other women have made the super-freaky-weird decision to have butt fat injected into their face. This is where we find ourselves. Our heads are up our own asses.

And I have a daughter. If I had a son, I'm sure I'd be taking issue with society in some other way. I can find something to be pissed about, believe me. But fate decided that I would be the mother to a little girl — and in a world like this, that's a tough job .

They say kids on average see about 55 commercials a day. We don't have cable, so I've cut this number down (at least in this house). But the message is everywhere: billboards, magazines, movies. I can't control the influx of every form of media. I can't stop every negative message. An easier alternative is teaching her the value of interpretation — a timeless lesson – and that she's good and beautiful just how she is.

I guess that's what I've done with myself at least. That is, of course, after struggling for years with eating disorders and a high-end lotion habit. I don't have money anymore for expensive face cream . So it is out of necessity, and not virtue, that I have come to the realization that wrinkles aren't that important.

Twenty-four million people struggle with eating disorders in the US. I don't want to play the blame game and assign sole responsibility for this epidemic to media in general. After all, they're just trying to sell mousse and skinny jeans. This is capitalism, people. We're about making money . And companies can't make money affirming who you are. Since I was a little girl, folks have been selling me the promise of acceptance through all kinds of products. It's expensive trying to keep up. But the more I dug for the answer of who I really am and worked tirelessly to give a thumbs up to that fleeting girl, the more I turned away from who those messages were telling me to be. I still forget a lot. And I still love mascara. I won't ever give it up. EVER. Unless, of course, I go blind from wearing too much mascara. Then it won't matter.

Point is this, there's an ideal somebody's been trying to give me for years. And only at 28-years-old have I been able to say, "No thanks." I guess Ava will have to brave the wild world herself. But before she leaves this house, I'll do my best to imprint these things on her sweet heart:

1. Be yourself.

2. Love yourself.

3. Wear the cardigan.

I feel like if I can raise her in such a way that even when her skin starts to sag she doesn't immediately go running to a syringe full of butt jello, I've done my job as a parent.

Same goes for me. I'm getting older, and I don't need to "be more." I just need to settle into who I am.

It's not the clothes; it's not the hair; it's not the skin. It's time. And that's OK.

26. BE NICE

Jesus Christ, slow down and be good to yourself for once in your life.

It's Friday and if you're reading this, it means your work week did not kill you and that there is indeed a Creator who loves us. There's vodka for those of you who party, and there's coffee for those who prefer inappropriate shaking to nausea. Cigarettes go to the lot of you! Except those who are concerned with living long, happy lives on a planet that's indifferent to your meaningless existence.

Kurt Vonnegut smoked unfiltered Pall Mall cigarettes for like, a hundred years or something. He was very unhappy about them not killing him sooner, or so he wrote. Oh, that wacky Vonnegut! God rest his pen. I recently decided that I would quit for my 30th birthday. I wish I could tell you that I'm logical and rational and that this is all about cancer, but it's really only part of it.

The other part is my skin. I look in the mirror and remember I'm not 18 on a pretty regular basis. They don't card me anymore, not even as a joke to make me feel good. You know how sometimes clerks will do that? And then both of you laugh? And then you say thank you and you walk off with the same feeling a great pair of jeans gives you? You know, right? Well they don't do that anymore. And I'm too old for cool jeans. Jesus, give me some khakis and a visor.

This brings me to my point. I should do some nice things for myself. Everyone should. I'm not that old and I work hard and I'm a human being on the planet...so, duh. Moms always carry the biggest cross. Teachers take a close second. I'm both.

But crucifying yourself is so uncomfortable and time consuming and anticlimactic. So I decided to skip the dramatics and just take that candlelit bath like I told myself I would...three weeks ago.

You have to schedule that crap, but do it. I'm talking to moms here: take the damn bath. You know how you love the park? Go there. Go there even if you think it's full of weirdos and rapists. Why do you think God made knives?

Buy some nice soap. Quit smoking. Do that for yourself. Tell yourself you're cool. Tell yourself you do a good job. Embrace your fallibility. Roll around it. Take the world off your shoulders for a minute and watch cat videos on YouTube. Do what you want.

Look Life and the world square in the eye and say, "You can't catch me. I smoke Pall Malls."

Wait. Say this instead: "I see you. Let's dance."

27. UGH. SUBURBIA.

How to survive a normal-person event when you're a huge fucking mess. But hold up, queen.

I could spend a lot of time setting this up, but I won't.

Humans are storytelling animals. I certainly like to tell myself stories, and more often than not, they're all just fancied tragedies. One of the prevailing ones is a narrative of failure. Certain situations summon this mean, inner narrator, and almost without me having to do anything, the story begins.

It's a tale I've told myself for a very long time, and it always ends with me feeling like I've been through an existential meat grinder. Such was the case on the day I lugged myself into the domesticated hell of Katy, Texas.

I had been invited to an 11-year-old's basketball game. I'm in a period of heightened emotional sensitivity, and I understand myself well enough to know this was going to be one of those experiences that have the ability to call forward that catty-ass narrator.

Maybe this sounds pathetic – the idea that I must mentally prepare for seemingly normal encounters – but it's true. And I decided I don't care what you think. I gave myself a lame, quiet pep talk, walked into the gym, knowing full well I might get weird about it, and took my seat.

I'm not shy about being non-traditional. In fact, I talk about it a lot. Maybe too much. Who cares? I was obsessed with the idea of normalcy for a long time, which was probably a product of my childhood. I spent half my life in a restaurant and diligently practiced the art of screaming as a form of communication. I used to be a hypochondriac, and I did that to get my mother's attention. It worked about 85 percent of the time.

We had a delightfully abnormal upbringing that I didn't appreciate until I got older. And for the record, my brain exaggerated most of the details and I'm convinced I have the very best parents on the planet. It only took me two and a half decades to figure that out.

When I graduated high school, I didn't go to college right away like books and movies told me I should. That was the American way, right? I was scared of classroom situations and found marriage to be another way to get out of the house. I met him April 15, 2004, got engaged two months later, and married him two months after that. I medicated myself with various chemical cocktails all throughout this time, spiraling ever downward. I went to jail. I almost died. I spent a Christmas in a mental hospital once.

Six months after my last drink, I separated from my ex-husband. I got pregnant. I got divorced. I gave birth to my daughter in 2009.

Here's what I did: I played a game of coconuts with major life events. I mixed them all up. The story I mentioned earlier emerged from this decade-long mess. I titled it: "I screwed up."

That paradox I lived in – the one where I idealized and wished for some self-constructed version of the American Way, while simultaneously living an opposite reality – doomed me to misery.

Sobriety did much to help me accept life as it was, but there was still some lingering guilt over the failures I assigned myself. They followed me like a shadow that only I could see – heavy and gray. When I'd go to church with my family for the holidays, the narrator would interrupt: "You screwed up."

At the private Baptist university I attended after I got sober: "You screwed up."

At parties, work, and the grocery store: "You screwed up."

As I watched a bunch of B-team kids shoot and miss every shot they took in this mecca of suburbia, I felt the narrator take a seat in my frontal lobe. She pulled out her usual book, the one with pages worn from constant flipping, and began recounting the same, nasty story she always did.

I looked down the row of chairs where all the cheering parents were seated. These people had life insurance policies; they lived on cul-de-sacs; they wore slacks **on the weekends**; they said things like, "bless his heart!" And when they laughed, they slapped their knees.

Across the street from the junior high gym, there was a high-end shopping center that looked like a wing of the Hogwarts School of Magic. The neighborhoods a mile away from this area had the names of the community plastered in cursive on the concrete walls of their entrances: "Pine View Ranch," "Silver Ranch," "Bring a Gun to Work Ranch," etc. They drove sedans and foreign

SUVs.

When this type of stuff is going on, I always feel like a little graffiti stick figure some bored kid added in the corner of a Norman Rockwell painting. I began to sink inside myself – something I like to do when I'm uncomfortable.

I was sitting in the epicenter of Normal – a drug addict, unwed mother, and perpetual washout. I remembered to smile though. I didn't want them to see the thousand-yard-shame-stare, lest I be removed from the game. I marinated in this suburban hell for nearly three hours when something suddenly, and thankfully, happened.

Before this unexpected moment, I'd always resented my non-traditional circumstances. I used them as a whip while alone in my house. Whoa, you don't need to call any hotlines. It wasn't every day. No one knew about it, save for a few close friends. To the rest of the world I screamed just a little too loudly how much I didn't care. "Let your freak flag fly!" This mantra is great, especially when it's authentic. Mine wasn't.

As shoes squeaked on the waxed floor of the gym, and parents (ALL COMPLETELY NORMAL OF COURSE) yelled positive slogans to their awkward, uncoordinated kids, everything in my soul decided I didn't want any of this. Ever. And this decision was sincere, unforced, and smooth. Some missing piece connected. That made-up American ideal – the one I outwardly repelled but inwardly desired – suddenly and uneventfully died.

The planets aligned just right and I snatched the book from the narrator. This one is long overdue for a rewrite.

And just like that, acceptance settled in on me. I liked myself. I really liked my weird, unorthodox life. And I didn't need to tell all those parents anything about it. I couldn't wait to get back to my ratty, little house behind the Dollar Store, the one with the turquoise walls and holes from when I used to drink (which I will finally fix with the paychecks from my new, big girl job).

I didn't want to turn my nose up and call them yuppies under my breath. I didn't want to prop myself up to look like them either. It was no longer a matter of being better than or less than. It was simply a matter of being different.

And it was okay.

Sometimes the earth's plates get caught against each other while dancing over the surface of the gooey mantle. The pressure mounts, shoving the hardened earth against each other in a war of organic strength. Physics decides the winner, and eventually the plates can slip past one another. The energy released in this process is what causes earthquakes. And stuff just falls into the earth during an earthquake.

Perhaps I was sitting on a fault line in Katy, Texas. I don't know why the epiphany came to me that day, or why it had come so peacefully. Usually my prophetic realizations come with more screaming. A plate slipped past another, and the story I've always told myself fell into the abyss. Good.

I'm rounding out this small piece of writing on my porch. My favorite tree on the planet is the one in my front yard. I can see a warm, yellow moon between its branches on this mild Sunday night. My daughter is asleep in the house. "Destruction" isn't a happy word, but I'm glad that story I wrote a long time ago is gone. I'm content, at least for this night, with my corner of the earth and how I came to be in here.

I suppose I can thank friction for this.

I only have one story, and some of it is actually true. Like I said, I'm up for a rewrite. This time I'm picking comedy. It's more fitting anyway.

28. THE OPPONENT AND ME

I wasn't born to feel shitty. I wasn't born to do something meaningless. I was born to slay.

Gah dang it, 32 is going to be my best year yet! Yes, I've had to come to terms with my gray hairs and wrinkles. I discovered another wrinkle the other day right between my eyes that looks like I'm permanently scowling. The only way to get rid of it is to look completely surprised, like I've just rolled up on a bear at a campsite. I've never actually seen a bear in the open before. Truth be told, the only bears I've ever seen in real life are the ones behind bars down at Baylor, which is probably why I have the damn scowl anyway.

I've been working out intensely since spring break of this year. In fact, I've done more physical exercise in the last four months than I've done in the last four years. I'm probably in the best shape of my life and I know that I could defend myself well in a cage fight.

But some opponents don't show up in a ring with wire around it.

And as I drove home today after a day of errands and mom things, I realized how fearless I have become. I wouldn't say reckless, because that implies a lack of thought. Oh no, this was all pre-meditated. I committed first degree murder on a life I did not want to live anymore.

I don't want to be a slave to fear and anger. I don't want to live average. I don't want to just get by. I want to run right out into the middle of the whole world screaming like Connor McGregor, maybe with my middle fingers flexed firmly at my adversity, and let everyone know I am here and I ain't scared of nothin'. Not anymore.

God has rounded me out into a good woman, I think. I do believe this is how God would have me live. Well, maybe without flipping the bird. But Lord knows, I ain't perfect!

I am grateful for all the rain and thunder I sat in before. I feel like I've lived several lives in my three plus decades on the planet. I had the childhood one, then the really stupid one. Then I had one where I pretended to be an adult who didn't drink, but was still miserable most of the time. I gave away a lot during that time. No one victimized me. I put a price on my head and let it all happen because the fear of the unknown was worse than the fear of staying.

But now, I'm as free as a bird. I'm not in any kind of relationship by my own choice. I take care of myself as best I can, and I'm thankful for my solitude most of the time. For once, I am not sinking my bubbling, exploding, white light energy into the deep abyss of a relationship formed out of need, rather than want. This means I do sugar scrubs on my face whenever I damn well please, and sometimes I talk to my dogs more than a person probably should - which is still ok.

I know that right now, as I sit here, I have the very best possible life I could have at this exact moment. I know one day it'll be different and I will be better for everything I've experienced in my whole life. Ever. It's always good if you choose to see it that way.

I hope you come to see it that way, too, if you don't already. Life is so grand and wonderful and painful and sad and beautiful. It's all a mess – a swirling, floating mess. And each day is an opportunity to look at that and say, "Yes, this is meant to be. All of it."

29. A CONVERSATION WITH GRIEF

It's like the Secret Garden, but not.

She thought maybe she would never wring out all those memories of long days she felt were wasted in a situation outside her control. Grief came to her as a childhood friend and sat beside her.

"You cry a lot, don't you? You hold a precious secret to win the love of stars, but you won't look up. You hold your old, worn story like the only matchbook at a campsite. It is protected somewhere in the back of your mind, behind cinderblocks and locks and rose bushes...

Your dreams are a smoky, blue fog that you swirl around in your tired hands. You keep yourself in your secret garden, away and alone. You sift through the gray words you wrote and make edits, and then I come to see you.

You wrote your story in chalk and the wind blew away your work. Here, take this. It's my best sharpie. Write your story with permanent ink.

Stop editing.

You're far too pretty to be bothered with leaky eyes and a slow heart."

Grief left her as gently as he had come. He eased his way through her ivy-covered gate, slowly. The girl held the sharpie in her right hand.

This is bold, she thought. And it was.

30. WHEN I AM OLD

A lot of shit doesn't matter.

Someday, when I am an old woman and I've given up on hair dye, I pray that my life will have been for some great purpose.

Someday, when I am an old woman and I don't pluck my eyebrows anymore because I've realized how meaningless it is, I hope people remember me as a light in a dark world.

Someday, when I am an old woman and I have accepted that stretchy pants are ok because no one really gives a damn anyway, I hope people see me as a human who ran the race so hard and so fast that her wipeouts were lessons for others, that her voice was a bullhorn for the mute, that her work was for the ones who felt too tired to move. I hope my agency is used wisely.

I hope that in my last years I am a worn book, my cover frayed from use and my pages smooth with a good story.

31. HEZEKIAH

Go for it!

Hezekiah loosened the rope from the pier and shoved off, grateful to have missed the splinters he surely deserved. His small, red boat faced a lacy sheet of glittering ocean laid out before the horizon.

As he was leaving for good and all, he turned to the shore and said the following:

"Ain't no man ever gained from lovin' the foothills when there's mountains behind 'em. I'm a simple man, patched together with time and mistakes and all kinds of wonderin' thoughts. I know where I been, and I don't care to stay here no longer. You been good to me, little island. Real good. But I best see what's out there, lest I perish on this here sand just a whisper of a man who didn't heed the call of a horizon that looked just a little too outta my reach."

32. TURKEY SANDWICHES AND BATTERY ACID

Spiritual truths aren't always easily discovered, but I will always look for one in a gas station sandwich.

This has been a long week. It's like if you stabbed a battery, once so beautiful and full of power, and then dripped its contents onto a thousand paper cuts between your fingers. Ugh. And then being bloated is also a thing right now.

Anyway, I was talking to a friend the other day about spiritual realities and awareness. There are, according to an author who I'm sure lives in Northern California or Boston or Key Largo or someplace like that, three realms.

There's the one that's completely legalistic, based on rituals. There's the one where you're out of order and feel uneasy because you're just not that into rituals anymore, so obviously you're doing something wrong because everyone knows the way to get God to love you is to lather, rinse, and repeat. And then the third is, you aren't ritualistic, and yet you know you're ok because your faith in God and evidence of that faith isn't contingent on any one set procedure.

I am somewhere between realm 2 and 3. Oh God, is this like an earthly purgatory where all I do is screenshot core workouts, pray, and eat gas station turkey sandwiches?

Speaking of that, there are few pleasures I delight in more than gas station sandwiches. There's a certain amount of fun about it all: "Ohhh, whose hands have been on this?....is this meat or...?...Please Lord, I really hope this is mayonnaise..."

And tonight, I made a split decision to eat a turkey sandwich from the Valero instead of the veggie chili I made last night. I got in my car and listened to music and reveled in my delicious risky undertaking. I went home and played the piano. I thought about where I've been. I wondered where I'm going.

Life is more than working and dying. When I wrap myself up from head to toe in the reality that spiritual truths are rarely discovered easily, that their discovery is what fires my engine, that sharing them is what moves me down the road – when I'm all in that, the world and its follies are really laughable.

My truths are mine, and they ride shotgun with me when I'm alone. I love them. I take care of them. Some of them I keep to myself. I enjoy them in secret...just like this turkey sandwich.

33. LOVE FIRST. TEACH SECOND.

Teachers are under-paid and over-worked. Hug them ASAP.

I hobbled like a freeze-dried zombie out of the stairwell to my room and ran into an Instructional Specialist in the hallway. She gave me "the look", nodded with a friendly laugh, and continued to her office. My first week teaching English at Cesar Chavez Middle School was over. It was 4:00. The hallways were a ghost town filled with hollow echoes of teachers and students. Before I left for the weekend, I visited the copier – my good friend – and used it as a pillow while sheets of poetry spit out the other end.

I didn't care about what was for dinner – only that it was human food and preferably fried. Or pure sugar. Or both. My feet were swollen from standing and walking. My brain was dead from thinking and monitoring. My voice was hoarse from talking over twenty other 11-year-olds. As my friend would say in Yiddish, I was "ongematert" – completely wiped out.

My mother is a teacher. I called her with my concerns about my students. Will they be okay later in life? This weekend? Are they okay now? Would I be able to help them get to where they need to be so they can be successful? Will the world snatch them up and take them away to some place "less productive"? If I have to be honest, I looked at my week-long assessment and was almost swallowed by the Self-Doubt Monster. Can I do this? I want to do this. Can I do this? I must do this. Can I do this? Can I?

My voice cracked and rattled. I cried, and I was okay with the deluge of emotion. It had been a long week.

She assured me, as an educator and not as my mom, that I felt no different than any other teacher since the dawn of time. This is what we're called to do. This is what we get to do. We show up to work at a place where The Future lives and breathes in living color: screaming in the gym, walking quietly in the hallway, and sitting in desks too small to contain the fullness of what they can be. We jump into content learning, and in the process, we all learn a little about what it means to be human. Especially me.

I am continually humbled at the honor to call myself "Teacher."

So, to those educators and administrators who survived their first week of school: way to go! To those who used the copier as a pillow and ate food that wasn't on their diet plan, because this week IT DOESN'T MATTER: it really is okay. To those who are new to the classroom, like me, that maybe saw a wink of doubt in your life's purpose/personal sanity: hold on. To all the above: thank you.

Yes, I can do this. And yes, you can do this, too. As we say at Cesar Chavez: "¡Sí se puede! Unido." Together, we can. Together, we will.

34. MUSINGS ON AN AIRPLANE

Me. Every time.

When the flight attendant is giving the safety briefing at the front of the plane, I almost always have to fight the impulse to yell, "Doesn't fucking matter! We'll all die anyway!" Because let's get real, if this plane goes down, the panic of my imminent death Is going to, oh I dunno, supersede my ability to think rationally about anything else and I'm not going to remember a damn word you just said.

So just like any other day in my life.

The only real likely scenario, outside all of us dying, is the idea that one of us might make it out of the wreckage and then have to implement survival skills to stay alive until a search party locates us.

So unless this piece of shit safety manual has some tips on how to make a shelter out of engine parts and leaves or how to kill bears with a sword fashioned out of smoldering plane wreckage, just save us all the hassle and fly this baby as fast as you can to our destination and keep that club soda a'comin'.

Yeah, and let's take a minute to talk about why the whole cabin of this plane smells like gas. I raise my hand, ever so gently, and a lady comes over. "Oh, I don't know what THAT is!" she says. "Well Babs, you better check it the fuck out because we're set for takeoff and I don't have a will."

VII.

POEMS THAT I DON'T CALL POEMS

35. CALLS

Heartbreak by gunshot.

Oh, this? This is the hole you gave me.

It's from when you opened my chest cavity with a shotgun blast.

It's nothing special, and it doesn't need any dressing. See? Ay, but a scratch!

Maybe an infection will clear it away.

It even hurts to breathe, but who needs air?

It's that stinging pain – the kind I get when I scrape my knuckles across the ground because I don't know which way I'm going and I forgot how to use my spine.

It's that kind of pain that rolls like thunder through all the fibers of my muscles, making waves from my bones to my tongue.

It all comes out as fury, only to leave behind withered skin and a sinking sadness that laps over the wound like small waves at low tide.

My mind twists and pulses in agonizing defeat because I can't be present like Eckhart Tolle asks and I can't be free like those preachers say.

But see, it doesn't need dressing. I'll be fine.

People don't ask me about it, in the same way many people don't ask someone missing a limb how that came to be their life.

It makes people double up with pleasantries. "You look good! How are you!"

That's never their actual question.

Their real question is: "Are you suicidal? Because if you're not, can we please talk about my wedding plans?"

And of course, I don't want to talk about it with them because they see the hole, and I've already explained it. And I want to be a good friend and keep all my blood to myself.

So I go to therapy. I sit in a small office with a down pillow on my lap, plucking the soft, white feathers out of microscopic holes and then I rub the cosmos-created velvet over my fingers.

It's calming to me, to so very gently destroy something belonging to someone else.

These fucking feathers aren't needle and thread, and neither is this nice, licensed man who patiently listens to me as I bleed out all over the office.

But see, it's really fine. I don't need any gauze or anything.

This pain becomes so regular that it goes in and out of a warm numbing underneath my sternum.

It's a heart attack all day, then like a hunter who startles its prey, it calms back down into the blind to wait.

This right here, this is the shotgun blast that hasn't killed me yet.

I'll be fine. It is but a scratch, but a transfusion would be nice.

36. BASEBALL BAT

Queen, you are a warrior.

Here we are in the good light of morning.

All the monsters are tucked safely away in the closet and under the bed.

We defeated them with sleep and breathing, and they won't bother us anymore.

We can look at all the rushing people and smile and tell them hello.

We can look them in the eye, even if it's scary.

We are tender-hearted, baseball bat slingin' slayers of fear and chaos.

We are pin-pricked and reminded of God and our place in the world.

We are people who pass you on the street.

Today is the day for laying all the pieces on the sidewalk so they might be warmed by the light,

Then fired in a kiln fueled by revolution to be fused back together into one.

37. GETTING OVER

The idea you need him is a delusion. Dryer sheets are the reality.

She straightened herself up because her Grandma gave her a spine. She said plainly, "Not to be rude, but I don't need you in my life."

And she mostly believed that.

But then there are times at the grocery store when his face materializes like fog in her head.

She shuts it off, grabs a bottle of toxic chemicals off the shelf, something she'll use to clean the house with later.

She's learned to do this. She has a switch that shoots up a steel wall between her heart and her brain.

But again, there he is. And then she remembers that lie he told and how he looked when he had been discovered.

He cowered on the floor at her feet, crying and banging his fists on the soft carpet.

She snatches a sponge, too. And floor cleaner. She knows she'll need it.

A thunderstorm boils up from some place she doesn't like to talk about.

It's not really her. She is spirit. She isn't rain.

Before things get too out of hand she grabs some more fucking dryer sheets – the expensive, perfumey kind because she is a woman who appreciates small, quiet luxuries.

He was a cheap rag who fell apart when dirt showed up. She affirms this. It keeps the water from boiling over.

And in her cart she carries all she needs to be new and made over.

She carries her world in her mind.

And when the families pass by shopping for school supplies, she just smiles.

Her lips curl because she knows she doesn't need him, and dryer sheets will make up the difference.

38. STOPPING BY

A little poem about exploding stars and being content.

Good Lord, just be content for once.
This is the only day I have to live.
This minute is all the cosmos has to offer.
Stars are exploding right now.
The sun is spitting flame into nothingness.
Everyone is at war.
Everyone is trying to make peace with something, too.
Somewhere, someone is falling in love.
Somewhere, someone is dying.
If I could see everything, maybe I could laugh a little more
at how small we all are.
Today is the day I've been waiting for.
Life is a bullet train and everyone's on board.
Don't worry about your baggage.
You won't need it where we're going.

39. BEFORE YOU THROW OFF YOUR CAPE OF SKIN…

All that there is and all that there will ever be is in today.

Today is the day you were made for.

Today means we are alive.

Today means there is still time to love people.

Your circumstances today were mapped out by Providence and an intricate dance of stars.

Today is a day for remembering the very miracle of being alive.

Don't you know that atoms vibrate, pulse, and waltz in and around you to make you whole?

You are a divine creation, equal to galaxies and supernovas.

You are the sky and the wind and the rain.

You are memory and love and kindness.

You are alive, and today means there's still time to realize this.

One day, I'll throw off this cape of skin.

I'll return to light.

One day, I'll pass from turmoil to eternity, from here to memory.

But today I am alive.

There's still time to realize it.

There's still time to wrap myself in breeze and my humanity.

It really is a miracle.

And this reality leaves no room for sadness or morose contemplation.

That's a miracle, too.

40. FOR A DRAGON

Started from the bottom now we're here.

Little dragon, my heart alive.
Whimsy and chaos and the world
Are all over you.
Take things in stride.
There's always a trade wind
That blows just for you.
Don't let yourself be mangled,
And if it happens anyway,
Remember that once,
You were but an acorn.
You sprouted from the gracious earth
And on her soil, you learn to be human.
You are the world, and the world is you.
Shine on, my swing bob chick.

VIII.

GOD IS NOT A SENATOR

41. AVOIDING GAY CONVERSION

This was published in a local paper and caused an uproar because no one in that town knew what satire was.

There are a hundred things to be afraid of in this country, but three take the lead. In reverse order of importance they are: economic collapse, robots, and gays. As American citizens, we have built a history on being proactive, being prepared, and being patriots. We may not be able to fend off an economic collapse, we may be too asleep to throw off all the insidious means by which this "president" is attempting to demolish democracy, but make no mistake, you can spot a gay from a mile away. The mass hysteria over their recruitment tactics holds some weight, and is worth the time it takes to read this in order to remain safely heterosexual. The lives of our children hang in the balance.

Homosexuals will try to convert God-fearing heterosexuals in a myriad of ways. The first, and one of the most seductive tactics, is simple kindness. If you must share a workplace with gays, avoid friendly greetings and casual water cooler talk. All it takes is one "hello" to engage in a conversation. Next thing you know, they're telling you about their cats, their custom built home, and the plight they experience, which is often over dramatized because that thing about drama queens is totally right. Do not be led astray. Their struggle is a result of foolish, lust-driven choices. Probably ones they made in college. Probably as a direct result of choosing to become an art major. Misplaced sympathy could spell disaster for you — disaster in the form of a partner named Frank or Midge.

Perhaps you have a gay family member. In this case, you will probably be invited to a fake wedding of some kind. This is one of the touchiest situations a heterosexual can find themselves in. These fake weddings are almost always completely fabulous and catered extremely well. They are full of drunken merriment and what appears to be sincere affection. Be careful. The wine, though aged and sweet, and the love shared, though authentic and glowing, is a trick to get you to believe that you, too, can have the best time of your life, if only you turn gay and permanently commit to Frank or Midge.

If you've already befriended a gay, obviously for the purpose of healthy reparative therapy, be sure to keep a good emotional and physical distance. Gayness can be passed on through a number of ways including knitting, salsa dancing, and talking. Your friend might disclose painful stories to you about rejection, alienation, and even violence as a result of being gay. These are textbook conversion maneuvers taken directly from the book little known to straight people titled, "Who's On First, Who's On Top: Creating a Super Gay Utopia in America." Avoid your gut instinct to empathize. Fight off the feeling that you must do something to help, the one that surely rings out in your heart when no one is around.

They will lure you in a number of ways. Men will saunter across dance floors with impossible grace and precision. They will bring all kinds of delicious, tiny pastries to parties. Women will help your recreation league softball team go undefeated for eighteen straight games. They will fix your motorcycle with lesbian witchcraft. One false move and the entire straight workforce of this country could turn queer. Imagine lawyers, housewives, airline pilots for God's sake, suddenly switching teams. Can you even fathom the danger of a mid-air gay conversion 30,000 feet above our amber waves of grain? God help us.

If we lapse on our responsibilities to protect heterosexuality and discourage gayness, we may open the door for a demographic with billions of dollars' worth of spending power to be able to flood money into our economy, thus further promoting their "Fire Island way of life." God, FIRE ISLAND. We may find ourselves on an equal civil rights footing with some of the most intimidating and well-dressed men in our society. Ladies will leave happy families to run off with Midge to start ranching in Wyoming. If you fear an economic collapse or the death of democracy, look no further than the ever-increasing army of gay people in this country. In this case, America's founding principle that all men (and women?) are created equal, and that we're all entitled to life, liberty and the pursuit of happiness must be ignored completely, lest Wyoming become overrun with lesbians and the entirety of Brooklyn be flooded with beautiful gay men. Let's face it – Brooklyn and Wyoming can't contain them all.

42. #RESIST

When a giant ass stands in the way of the world and what is right, you mount up. Regulators!

I bet in other places people wake up and think, "Today is Wednesday." Waking up on any day in the Trump era, however, is like coming to in a kiddie pool filled with jello. Every. Single. Day.

You aren't entirely sure how you got there and you damn sure know it wasn't your intention. But anyway, so you're covered in the jello (so you hope), and you look around and try to find someone who has a better idea of the story. But all you see are other people covered in jello. It's like a scene from fucking Ghostbusters. All over the place. Some people are like, rubbing the jello all over themselves, so happy they've found this piece of heaven. They scowl at you when you ask for the story and tell you you're un-American for wanting to wake up in bed like a normal human being.

But others look as confused as you. They look worried, mostly because they really, really hope their friend that drove them there is still around so they can get home.

And then you vaguely remember that your special friend did in fact leave with Tom Hanks, Oprah, and a billionaire to go kite surfing on a yacht in the South Pacific. But yeah, a lot of people are just walking around trying to figure out how the fuck to get home.

You think, "Lord, if I make it out of here, I swear I will never, ever drink Long Island Ice Teas during an election year ever again."

And a little in the distance, you see a little gathering of blue, green, and red slimy people. They have these lost expressions and dark eyes. You immediately know, "That's them. That's my tribe."

As you walk over to the safety of the group you hear the sound of what you think must be the angel Gabriel's trumpet. "Christ! God no, it's the second coming and here I am, JUST AS I KNEW I WOULD BE, covered in whatever the hell this is, trippin' on kiddie pools!"

But no, it's the party's host. He stands on a raised platform looming over the wobbling, terror-stricken mass of rainbow ooze people. He is orange, and he likes the slime. Oh, he loves it. His bleached white teeth cut through the patches of orange, wrinkled skin. You know — you just know — he is the one who put that shit in your drink. He is dangerous. And he drugged all your friends, too.

Wait, is it just another fucking Wednesday?

Lord knows, this isn't a polite political climate. What's right will always be right. Oppression and discrimination will always be wrong. Jello is good for two things: diets and retirement homes. When you wake up in the shit and there's another hard rock thrown at a marginalized group, you have to wipe your hands on the gritty earth and say, "Hey asshole! No!"

And you take your hands and use them to grab the hand of another. And all of you lock arms and take a sharp aim at the orange, slimy host standing behind a podium he created for himself.

We fight and we take care of each other. We may have not intended to come to the party, but we sure as hell wake up here every day. We will make it together. Always remember, we take care of each other. There's enough soap for all of us when we finally make it home.

43. I ABANDONED RELIGION FOR LOVE'S SAKE

This was written before the Supreme Court's decision to legalize same-sex marriage. God loves gay people, guys. So quit being dicks about it.

Several days ago, I watched a video of a local pastor outlining a plan of action regarding what he called the "homosexual issue." Usually I get angry at things like this. But on this occasion, I didn't start foaming at the mouth and steaming at the ears. I just sat there, almost like I had been suddenly surprised and unable to respond. I felt something unfamiliar. I felt...heartbroken, terribly sad, and overwhelmed.

I am in no way bashing this man. His beliefs are sincere to him, ones he keeps closer than anything. I'm sure that his faith, his religion, and his God are the most important aspects of his life. They certainly are of mine. I do, however, believe his philosophies cause harm. Dogma blinds humble servants, and he is a humble servant, no doubt.

"The homosexual issue." He said it like it was the "poverty issue" or the "teen pregnancy issue." Like it was a condition or circumstance that could be solved by implementing resources and maybe doing a little creative problem solving.

What?

And I thought, for whom is this an "issue"? It's not hard to figure out that he meant, on a small scale, his church, and on a larger scale, THE CHURCH. Which

144

church? The Christian church. But hey, we're all even somewhat conscious of the fact it's 2015 and we already knew that.

His video runs 20 full seconds before he quotes the first scripture. This is to be expected because he's a pastor and not an astronaut, or a baker, or an Amway salesman. Yes, he is a pastor – a man who received thousands of dollars' worth of religious training at... at... well, I couldn't find any information on where or if he received higher-level education, other than a business degree from Baylor in the 80s.

Anyway, I watched the video, and I got sad. His main message concerned the impending Supreme Court decision on same-sex marriage. In his words, that decision "will not only hurt people in a devastating way, but it will also cause an adverse effect for us as people of God. If we just have the opinion or the desire to believe that marriage is between a man and a woman, or to believe that unique male and female is the way God created us – if we simply make that stand, that could be even illegal in our nation."

No. The Supreme Court ruling in favor of same-sex marriage would not mean that your opinions are illegal. I could step outside to the corner of Washington and 5th right now, wearing a rainbow two-piece and a purple wig, holding an early 90s era jam-box blaring Ton Loc, and yell at the very top of my lungs:

"I hold the opinion that gay marriage should be super-duper legal!"

...and none of that would be against the law. Bringing that much funk to downtown might catch me a citation for disturbing the peace, but my beliefs and opinions would be entirely untouchable. Duh. This is America and not Communist China.

Moreover, the traditionally-held opinion that same-sex marriage should be/remain illegal does, in fact, hurt people. When same-sex couples can't receive the same benefits as heterosexual couples – benefits like health insurance and spousal rights in emergency situations – those two human beings do suffer. There are far too many cases of couples having to endure tremendous strife and heartbreak during already trying times because their marriages were not considered legal.

The opinion that same-sex marriage should be legal does not in *any way whatsoever* infringe on the rights of heterosexual couples or even a church's ability to function in the way it so chooses. They may miss out on several fabulous wedding deposits because of their beliefs, but it won't bar them from being able to worship or pray or get non-profit status. It won't put them out of business, and I don't anticipate mobs of gay men storming the door of local churches with glitter and strobe lights. So really, it'll be ok.

And again, these are just opinions we're talking about here. Those are never illegal. If they were, half the country would be rotting in jail for not liking Obama. Opinions don't mean anything in the grand scheme of things. What does matter is legislation. And if you want to get right down to it, outlawing same-sex marriage has a very tangible negative effect on the lives of millions of Americans. It's not a theory. For many, it is their reality.

After I watched the video again, just to make sure I heard everything right, I started thinking about the God I believe in, the Bible, my friends who are gay, and what all of this means. I cannot stand with a religion that says, "Jesus loves you exactly the way you are...now change." I'm thinking of a guy I know. I wonder if he doubted the authenticity of the words when he sang, "Jesus loves me this I know, for the Bible tells me so." If he didn't then, I wonder if he does now.

Suddenly I was standing at the edge of a great, spiritual precipice. I began to cry, then outright weep. I laid my head down on my desk and let tears fall in my lap. My heart shattered. How cruel it is to use such a formidable weapon against people, to suggest that who they are is outside God's love and favor – to say that they are "not right," they are broken, and they are innately defective. For the Bible tells them so.

God's love is not to be used as a tender battle axe.

The God I choose to believe in made all of Creation the way it is. It wasn't an accident, and homosexuality is not a choice. It was in that moment of thought that a great schism occurred, leaving nothing but a gulf filled with unpalatable dogma.

It was there and then that I decided to part with religion. I was given the opportunity to develop a relationship with God as I understand Him (Her, It, etc.) when I got sober. And I guess the God I believe in is different from that pastor's God. I feel like it's my job from now on to remind my LGBTQ friends whenever they might hear something as soulfully painful as the message I've been discussing that there aren't any accidents and they are loved equally by our Great Creator.

And just as important is the continuous work of making *de jure* discrimination a memory for the LGBTQ community, so that they might have an opportunity to live and thrive in the way humans should. We all have the right to life, love and the pursuit of happiness – all of us – gay or straight.

For the Declaration of Independence tells me so.

44. DON'T FEED THE CHRISTIANS

Religious people need not be feared — only well-watered, well-fed, and understood.

When my oldest brother was an infant, my parents decided to join a church so that he would have religion in his life. They have stayed members of the same church for nearly thirty years now, a much larger Baptist church than the ones they grew up in. We have never been an overly religious family, but throughout my childhood, we maintained consistent Sunday morning attendance, and each kid was baptized at some point by the same pastor.

Growing up in this church, I always felt like an outsider looking in, like someone merely passing through to be viewed but never known. Words from the Bible twisted up in my mind and I created a warped, terrifying view of the Christian God which I fled from at the earliest opportunity. This was the context under which I ventured away from the church house, leaving behind all those well dressed, holy people. After all, they and I were only there to view each other from our respective posts in the pew, not to get to know each other as fellow travelers.

Christians, as a result, became like inhabitants of an exhibit at the zoo, with placards of misinformation written with my own hand in crayon, glittery pink gel pen, and black sharpie. "Look here, the Christians, residents of Stupid Town. It says they feed on judgment and the weak. Their natural habitat remains the brick and mortar houses of ridged doctrine, and their population has dwindled because of the plague of hypocrisy." This exhibit is boring. Let's move on.

The whole time I never realized I was segmenting a portion of the population as backwoods freaks of nature, characterized by exclusive teaching and kooky fundamentalist tradition – a separate mass of weirdo people, wholly different in their mental and spiritual makeup. They were huddled behind thick glass, and I had neither a place among them nor any interest in knowing them as human beings. I stayed this way for about ten years.

Long story. Lots of events. Fast forward....Baylor. The pristine, manicured campus of one of the largest private Baptist universities in the country is where my feet landed on an August morning in 2011. A school where mission trips are endless and chapel is mandatory - a faith community in its finest threads.

Again, the thick glass and the feeling of being a different type of weirdo among thousands of other super weirdos. I wasn't like them, and that was okay. Nonetheless, I considered myself a spiritual person and there was something to be said about entering a faith community. If power wasn't felt person-to-person, the air surrounding campus felt infused with something divine, and that in itself helped me along many days when I felt too tired or bitter to walk.

While in my first year at Baylor, I got a view from a different angle of the exhibit I constructed so long ago. Still confined, I took more notes and did more research. Still in Stupid Town I see. Press on, brothers and sisters.

One of my biggest struggles has been reconciling Christian teaching with my innate Universalist leaning.

How do I believe in the resurrection and have Jewish friends at the same time? Is there a chapter and verse I haven't found yet? John 14:6 arouses a multitude of questions. No one comes to the Father except through Him? But what about those left outside the boundaries of this faith - those in the netherworlds of Buddhism, Judaism, and those especially wild, crazy and "misguided" Hindus? That seems to me like a disproportionate and cruel amount of people to be cast needlessly and callously into the fires of Hell simply for not agreeing with one line in one religious text. That is, if Hell even exists.

Personally, I think God is all the same Guy, no matter what organized religion happens to be talking about Him. Dare I say this openly in the church I grew up in? I lack the boldness of the saints to do it publicly, but I say it in private around small kitchen tables. Press on, brothers and sisters.

This brings me to the meat of the story. I love people who hold a deep passion and belief in something, jaywalkers and serial killers excluded here. The capacity of the human heart and mind to hold a cemented conviction of some noteworthy cause is fascinating and hopeful.

So, when I was leaving Rollo's the other day and ran smack into the two fellows I always see lugging a cross up and down Valley Mills Drive, I felt moved to roll down my window and ask them what the hell their story was. I called them over and they were all too thrilled to have to an opportunity to talk.

"Why do you guys do this? Why walk with this cross up and down the street? Some of this seems obvious, but what is your personal reason for doing it?"

And without missing a beat, the man launched into his tiny speech:

"I was sitting in my house one day and I was praying and I said, 'God, I just don't feel like I have what those other people have. I'm sort of done with all of this I think. I don't have any use for it.' And then I saw something, like I was watching TV, and it was me on the cross. I was hanging there, and Jesus came and scooped me up like a little kid, took me down and held me in his arms just like he was a big dad. And He told me He loved me so much and that He died for me so that I didn't have to. So, I walk up and down the street hoping someone will ask me about it, just so I can have the chance to tell them that God loves them so, so, so much."

That was a rough paraphrase of what the man said. Of course, by this point I was crying a little, mainly because I'm emotionally hyper-sensitive and also because I really believe he had that experience. He went on a little more about some general things about his life, gave me the contact information for his wife in case I ever wanted someone to talk to and invited me to a life group at his church.

And of course he offered to pray for me which I gladly accepted, because I don't care what God you pray to, I will always take a prayer. I thanked him for sharing his story with me and away the two men went, soldiering on down the road spreading their version of truth and light and hope.

It was a magnificent thing to see two people so

floored by their belief in *something* – and they weren't even waging war about it.

I empathize with spiritual skeptics when they express bitterness about Christian hypocrisy, evil motives and the like. I have had and still have discussions centering on that topic - had one just yesterday, which prompted this writing.

I won't say that the cage I built for people like those men came tumbling down after they left, all my doubt cleared away, a rainbow appeared, and my soul sang a song of clarity. No, no. None of those things happened. But I ripped a few of the bars off. A little more of the glass shattered. There wasn't so much distance between the Church and me, and this wasn't because I found the magic scripture to cure the doubt/doctrine blues. It was because I had taken a small amount of time to ask this cross totin' man about his story.

He wasn't just someone in the pew next to me. He wasn't just some deacon somewhere. He was just another human being, compelled to act on his faith, and I had talked to him. Turns out, they're not all the same.

The impressions I held were self-constructed, always had been. Even though I knew it long before this encounter, I felt it again after a long absence. I knew a few cool, churchy people once before. They invited me into their home when I was all knocked up and fed me a few times, but I felt awkward in their group (my baby bump was not a result of Immaculate Conception). That isn't their fault of course. And they were the first to dispel the rumor that all people of faith were ridged wet blankets.

Can you believe they had senses of humor and one of them even said "ass" one time? I thought that was against the rules or something. I still think of them fondly.

I keep my spiritual walk fairly personal, talking about it with only a few friends and the entire Internet occasionally. I identify as a Christian in some regards, disagree with other things, but for the most part I take a Universalist approach.

If when I die, I'm sent to a sort of Half-Hell, I'll write you guys a postcard and tell you I was all wrong. Until then, I'll keep an open mind and just stick to doing the next right thing, whatever that is. And I will fail often and remember I'm human. I will say more prayers and try again. Maybe I'll sit cross legged and meditate for a few months, maybe I'll take a keener interest in nature, and maybe I'll attend a church service or two.

But no matter what, I'll be digging deeper into this idea that the universe is more than physical matter. There is a divine flow through me and all things, and my job isn't to figure out what or who is right, but to DO what is right while I'm here. That seems to be easier, and probably what the Spirit of the Universe wants me to do anyway.

I think most all religious teachings can agree on that. My questions will persist and in the search for the answers I'm sure I will grow into a more wholesome human being...at least I hope I do. I'd hate to expend all that intellectual energy only to come up empty handed. That would sure be a waste, something that would really piss my rotting corpse off.

The big epiphany that may not mean anything to you,

dear reader, is that I realized a little more the significance of horizontal spirituality – the concept that through interpersonal communication we learn more about and grow more in a holy relationship with that Supernatural Thing that exists outside the world's understanding.

Since you guys are the only ones I ever really see anyway, it's nice to know we can all learn from each other. Press on, good brothers and sisters, travel well, do good work, and I'll catch you on the flip side...wherever the hell that is.

45. PALM OIL PRAYER

When the world is so big and your oars aren't big enough to fend off hurricanes.

God,

Help me to see others as people, not enemies.

Help me figure out what products I use that contain palm oil so I can get rid of them because it's killing orangutans.

Help me to go to sleep tonight, even though I know we are 100% destroying the entire planet and each other.

Help me to get rid of stuff I don't need, so I can have room for what matters. This includes emotional baggage.

Help me be kind to people I don't like because I think their opinions are idiotic. Kindness will help them see more than hatred.

Help me to not compare myself to things I see on Facebook and Instagram, because no filter will cover brokenness.

Help me to realize we are all stranded here in the same sinking ship, and we are all trying to make it back to the same shore.

And let me have a cool dream tonight. No murder-warehouses again. Thanks.

And amen.

46. I'LL LEAVE YOU WITH THIS

A closing remark or two.

If you'll indulge me a moment, I have something I want to say to you. Here, is this your soap box? Mind if I borrow it a minute? I won't be long. Just let me get this microphone and T-shirt gun. Ok, I'm ready now.

Humans are the strangest creatures on the planet, even more strange than the Naked Mole Rat, which is what comes up if you google "strangest creature on the planet." To be honest, I think the Hagfish has a few things on the Naked Mole Rat, but who am I to judge creepy animals? You think the Hagfish gets upset at itself? You think the Naked Mole Rat ponders all the steps it's taken in its life and regrets its mistakes? You think the Polyclad Flatworm worries about whether or not it's okay to wear adult footie jammies? Hell no, they don't.

We were blessed and cursed with the ability to reason. We run around and become obsessed with things like monogramed hand towels; we quit jobs; we divide and hurt each other. But, we also fall in love. We know what it's like to sit under the stars, paralyzed by glory, and think about how we must have got here and where we are going. We learn to crave hope and joy and faith. We get to taste the victory that only comes from being fired in the kiln, which yes, does often taste like ash. It must be that way.

If we clung strongly to monsters we perceived as saviors, we'd be much worse off. Sometimes my monsters are people, and sometimes they're Fear and Greed and Jealousy and Anger. The kiln has a funny way of removing that vicious debris. Thank God for those little plane crashes I had that burned away what wasn't necessary anymore, so that I might find joy in the rest of this life.

What I've learned in the kiln is everything is going to be okay. No matter what.

Life is not misery and pain and destruction, though sometimes those are on the menu. Life is a never-ending explosion of atoms, a symphony of love and mercy and grace, a monumental expedition of the human spirit. Roberto Benigni was right: Life is beautiful.

I heard somewhere that laughter is the music of the cosmos. Ain't that the truth? I bet if I could sit still long enough, I'd hear the stars giggle at all of us running around here trying to be remembered for something. Shakespeare was right, too: it really is much ado about nothing.

So let's not set out dainty cups and pretty doilies for our pity party. Take down the balloons and cancel the cake order! Rip up the guest list because no one sent in a RSVP anyway! Do it! Go through your life, your mind, your spirit. All the little whoopsy daisies, the rolled ankles, the rips and tears, the fender-benders – all of these – these are ours! Claim them! Be thankful they happened! If you're a long way from that feeling, keep rowing. You'll get to the shore on the other side soon enough. These things are kindling for our fire. The kiln takes care of the rest.

I've been sitting at a typewriter for some time now, writing fiction and nonfiction about myself and all of you. I used to be very uncomfortable about the story my pages told. I was embarrassed. I was ashamed.

I used to tell boyfriends that I was a busted car in the

back of a lot, and I had a bad Carfax report. There were two big accidents on my record, but the body was still nice and I still had grit for a few more hundred thousand miles. This was the pathetic, sad sell of myself to others.

Then I realized there's nothing wrong with my story. It's mine. I own every word of it. Good luck getting me to shut up about it. If we aren't honest with each other about our stories — even the secret parts — how can we help others who have similar ones? Be loud. Be audacious. Roll your neck if you have to.

Never forget how mighty you are, and always remember we've slayed dragons. Humans have been doing it for years. I wouldn't call fighting a pastime, but wars have always brought many unexpected things to me. War has helped me find God, and in finding God, I have found myself. So it is with us all. Go tell someone about your war. Share your victory.

Let's soldier on together from now on.

ABOUT THE AUTHOR

She woke up one day on her drooping mattress with the blessed resolve one only finds at the bottom of a hole out of which they're willing to climb. She put on her old shoes, but they felt new. Then she went and bought a badass multivitamin and decided to change her life.

Susan Duty is a writer of various forms. She writes because that's what makes her feel good. She will fight to the death over the importance of the Oxford Comma. She knows you have a gift, and she believes you should share it.

In her lifetime, she has been the manager of a pizza joint, a drunk, a teacher, and a dreamer. She is 32-years-old and lives with her daughter in the mecca of weird people: Waco, Texas.

81247296R00102

Made in the USA
Lexington, KY
14 February 2018